## Reactions

Abandon all preconception and luxuriate in Lorri Jack. This poet loved language. She nurtured it, protecting it against the often harsh elements of her life. What we end up with in this heartbreaking collection is a portrait of a woman under thirty who was as much an artist as she was an outlaw. Through her intricate evocations of time and place, we can smell the bad coffee, see the dirty streets, and imagine that she is still here writing for us, telling us something new about an era long gone that she was both wary of and in love with.

*Deborah Pintonelli,* poet,
author of *Meat and Memory* and *Ego Monkey*

I know a poet has chops when half-way through a 100+ page collection, I am energized by envy and inspired to compete. Lorri Jackson is a poet who makes me want to write poems while knowing I could never reach her glorious heights or startling lows and that it doesn't matter, that writing is all that saves us and the words are all we need to leave behind. Lorri Jackson's book *So What If It's True* did just that to me. Her language is gritty and gorgeous, her sensibilities stunning and exceptional. Jackson is a poet in the ilk of Patti Smith, Rimbaud, an impossible bastard child of Dylan Thomas mated with Bukowski and Joni Mitchell. Jackson's language is blunt, garrulous, self-deprecating, insightful, cruel, and painfully honest. Her work soars and dives and takes the reader along for the ride. She leaves behind in *So What If It's True* evidence that a unique and troubling genius was extinguished by a needle prick, leaving only "…the red wail of sirens / hoses hissing / the coach house smoldering / smoking / and me, perhaps found / unrecognizable, a little / twisted and curiously / dead." Like Christopher Marlow, who died far too young from a self-inflicted life outside of his astonishing writing, Jackson leaves behind a body of unfinished potential we can only mourn as lost to all of us. I closed this necessary book wondering what would have happened had Jackson lived to carve her complete story into the bark of the American tree. *So What If It's True* belongs in any thinking person's desert island collection.

*Joani Reese,* poet, educator, author of *Night Chorus*

# SO WHAT IF IT'S TRUE

FROM THE NOTEBOOKS
OF LORRI JACKSON

*Edited by RW Spryszak*

THRICE PUBLISHING

Thrice Publishing
PO Box 725114
Roselle, IL 60172
**ThricePublishing.com**

So What if It's True — From the Notebooks of Lorri Jackson
All work copyright ©2017 by LeAnn Jackson Bigos unless otherwise
noted.

Book Design by David Simmer II and Thrice Arts

First Thrice Publishing Edition: May 2017

ISBN10 - 1-945334-01-0
ISBN13 - 978-1-945334-01-6

Printed in the United States of America

Photo of Lorri Jackson by Fred Burkhart
Property of Larry Oberc, used with permission

Part of a letter to Chris Peditto – July 13, 1987


When i can get my mind settled i want very
much to begin working on a manuscript...
is it for the ego tripping part, to want
a book, not a fancy book, not an overpriced
book that will join the ranks of all the
rest. Ive got beginnings of enough stuff,
tangible object of the sweat guts blood
gone into the woods trying to explain this
existence. and ive only scratched the
surface, that is the part that constantly
numbs me, that theres so much more to say
explain. and a collection of my best would
say more in its entirety than a few isolat-
ed pieces found in small publications here
and there. only thing is i don't know where
to start...

                    Lorri

# Where To Start

There have been two other attempts to put a collection of Lorri Jackson's work together that I know of. Both went down in flames. I don't know why. But it seems that every time someone wants to re-open this story all kinds of shit starts to happen. Some people hide. Some people stand up. Others go dark altogether. There were hard feelings. Lamentations. Sorrow. Twenty-six years have gone by and there are still people who have a version to tell. In his December 1990 obituary for Lorri in *Letter eX* Barry Cassilly talked about the "dramatically severe persona by which most people in Chicago got to know her." Forces of nature are like that.

Face it. Lorri died in 1990 at the age of 28. She suffocated after injecting heroin. The article in the *Chicago Tribune* said she died "on a stranger's couch." And the reporting police officer said what he found on her "wasn't poetry... it was nonsense." Oh right. Who knew we had a laureate genius in the thin blue line?

But the newspaper article and Lorri's final hours it described are not her story. Though we can't escape the references, and at times her work is painfully full of them, this collection is not a glorification of, or a misplaced romanticism for, a somehow grand and noble dissipation. There is no romance to it. *Sid and Nancy* was not a musical comedy.

It's just what happened, and it's the last we'll speak of it.

Instead, let's recall Chicago in the late 1980's. The Reagan/Bush years. Otherwise known as the start of the Great Dumbing Down. The birth of the long trickle down lie. We don't have cell phones. We write on typewriters. Most of them are electric. People laugh about Young Urban Professionals. You know the term. But there is an undercurrent. Like orphans under the viaducts smoking cigarettes, near narrow jazz clubs at 2AM. Neo is still down an alley. Exit keeps punk alive. Cabaret Metro is in full stride. You can find everything in Chicago from Art Blakey and the Jazz Messengers to the nascent evolutions of the Red Hot Chili Peppers when they're in town.

There's Oz. There's The Green Mill. And a tavern in my old neighborhood converted from a family-owned, working class drinking hole into something called The Get Me High. Bucktown. Where none of us can afford to live anymore.

The alternative press, so called by choice because of its stand against the larger and exclusionary forces of big money publishing, runs on a true subterranean pulse. And a wide range of these publications, mostly funded out of pocket or sometimes backed by a local college or small arts grants, are accepting the work of a poet by the name of Lorri Jackson with rapid regularity.

Some of her material was translated into German and published there with *Kozmik Blues*. Here in the states you could read her work in *The Chiron Review*, *Alpha Beat Soup*, *Tomorrow Magazine*, *Clutch*, *letter eX*, *Black and White*, *Nothing Sinister*, *Hollowpoint*, *Vice Versa*, *Heat Press*, *A New Geography of Poets*, *The Fiction Review*, *New American Writing*, *Derailed*, *Painted Bride Quarterly*, *Guts*, *Long Shot*, *The Columbia Review*, *New City*, and so many others – some with lifespans so fleeting we can't even remember their names.

If you knew your way to the venues, you could also hear Lorri perform her work around town. She read in big halls and small rooms. In dank taverns and one-light stages. Club Lower Links, Gaspar's, and so many transient venues that were in on the birth of the Slam. Remember the famous night she lit a stink bomb in the middle of one of her readings? Yeah. There were a hundred thousand people there, apparently. And more every year.

Lorri had been an opening act for Henry Rollins. Worked with the band Skatenigs. Did voice collaborations with Al Jourgenson of Ministry. Was about to go on a national tour with performance artist Lydia Lunch. She had collections of poems published or about to be published. *Scat*, *My Mouth Is A Hole In My Face*, *Seriously?*, *New Logic For New Sores*, and more. She knew what she had going. She had to know. And she was being mentioned with more and more frequency in upmarket conversations.

That's when the rug got pulled out.

> *I didn't slam a predictable door when I left*
> *& funny how these hooded winking streets*
> *no longer worry me*
> *as their threat becomes my comfort.*

My connection to her is that she sent a version of "*And The Corpse Had Numerous Tattoos*" to my magazine the day she died. Well. Both stories ended the same way. You can read the version I published near the end of this collection. I was the unwitting recipient of a hard coincidence. It's not something you forget.

•

This collection was mostly culled from Lorri's notebooks and archives held by the Jackson family. It's not the whole deal.

The archive we worked with contained letters, revised pieces and notes Lorri made on her poems and prose work. We had to work out a few things. Her poem *My Life As A Big Fat*

*Pig* has more than one version. Her most notable fiction, *And The Corpse Had Numerous Tattoos,* is known to have several iterations. We find one part of that work presented in her archive as a poem. There is another version of it with another ending. Perhaps still another. It was in both poetry and fiction forms. Which was which? No one is completely sure. Most of the material is just as it emerged, other things were clearly intended to be improved upon.

But to this day no one is sure if everything she did can even be found. People who have scattered versions of things in their possession are – for their own reasons – unwilling or unable to share them. Lorri posted poems to telephone poles in Louisville under the banner of *Draft: Louisville Poets,* and left them there. Do we have all of those? We can't tell. All the failed attempts to create this kind of collection in the past may have ended up dispersing both published and unpublished material, even original copies, to the seven winds. A complete collection may not ever be possible. Or is it? Nobody really knows. We'll never know. Probably we're not supposed to know.

And there were choices that had to be made in the creation of this collection. Some harder than others. The presentation is not done in chronological order. Attempting to correct some editing errors is always a question of lines you are crossing. Because we can see active revisions in her notebooks, it is safe to assume that some of the material would have likely received some measure of revision from her at some time or another. Other things are left as is. Frozen as they came out.

We also had what Lorri mentioned more than once as what she considered her best and most favorite, *Gone/Flesh/Wise.*

•

Though she was separated from them by decades, a connection to the Beats (Kerouac, Ginsberg, Carr, Burroughs) runs strong in her work. Her contemporaries mentioned this at the time too. Sometimes her words seem scooped out of the same stream as Kerouac's *On The Road* or Ginsberg's *Howl.* And at no time are they any less dark, whether in prose or poem.

> *What if everything fell down*
> *and fell down hard, all the walls*
> *of buildings & warehouses*
> *rows & rows of files & files*
> *crashing all around*
> *the banners of their lies and slogans*
>      *useful now only as slingshots*
> *and blankets*

Not a feminist by her own admission or in some strict philosophical sense they have notwithstanding, rightfully claimed her. And well they should, because she called the shots. She was frank about her sexuality. She was frank about her needs and wants. Her fears and nightmares. She was frank about everything. She was a lot of different things to a lot of different people. They told the world. She was good. She was bad. She was careful but wild. Cynical. Unforgiving. Often hilarious. Aggressive and vulnerable. Insightful. Self-destructive. Competitive. Sometimes compassionate. Angry. Funny. Cutting. Always quick. A little dangerous. Gentle once you got past the rough layers. Spiritual. Total Street. Mixed up. Focused. Stone blind to what she was getting herself into, but clear-eyed and chilling about the end of it all. She mentions to Chris Peditto that good things happen in October. Writes a poem with deadly overtones about October. Sends a piece to a magazine that seems to be a vision of what was going to happen to her later that very night. In October.

There is terror and grace in here. The hard and the soft. That which is real, and that which is only imagined. And all of it can be found in the words. All those things. They're all right here, firing out of every poem. Every sentence.

•

What attracts people to the work still, and what has always

attracted, is her way of moving with the unexpected and true, often in a form we're not always ready for, even if she has to invent or dissect a word to make it stick. We find this over and over.

And what is contained in this collection is nowhere near the sum total of Lorri's output. There is more. Much more. Enough for a second volume? In quantity, yes. But these are the best. We'll see what happens down the road. Lorri's work might deserve a larger stage than this. I can't deny that fact. But, for now, let's just make sure to answer her question in the letter we presented at the top of this show.

This is where to start, Lorri. Right here.

One can only guess what she might have made if she had come along with us all to where we are now. Sadly, that's part of the fascination, I suppose.

> *all this shuffling from place to place*
> *is pointless, all*
> *this drifting leaves a sticky film*
> *clinging to my memory. i need*
> *to sit and sort out all my lives*

Personally, I'd rather something else was true.

RW Spryszak

Photo of Lorri Jackson by Fred Burkhart
Property of Larry Oberc, used with permission

# Contents

**Used with permission. Copyright Oyster Publications.
These and much more of Lorri Jackson's work available at
*etsy.com/shop/OysterPublications* — Thanks to Lainie Duro

## Rim

this might be
my life, with all
its misspellings, an
afternoon
of wheelchairs, the work bins
mixed, missing humboldt park
yearnings, so what if it's true
that i wanna live in cheap hotels
easy to get, easy to forget
surrounded by blue
old men, the end spread out
and floundering in the present
faded ink beneath the skin
forearms resting
on nothing

## House of Selected Flames

The mind is at least one room.

A headlight beam reaches into the walls
then escapes out the window
after just one touch. A passing affair
being coarse and shot with the idea
of love with a dark wall. I have nothing
to say. The light runs
leaving a vague taste of the Highway.

In my mouth color fades. the jujubes
of November & white bear icicles
close in tight on August. Come back
here. Can I tell you how unbearably cold
this room is? Everything freezes. I am
a winter sun, pale and orange across the floor
in the weakest tribute, in the loveliest ache.

What I am trying to say is this: your house
is very lovely. It has many bright hallways
& rooms leading downward
to you. I am in the back,
behind Sunday mornings and gleaming windows
of pineapple and yogurt, rich New Orleans
coffee, & the New Yorker
Down the hall I am behind
dinners at diners on Friday night
with best friends from college
& major publications,
behind the hours your wife is home
from the office, the spa, from school
where she takes classes at night
behind the sofa, in the closet, hiding in
the bathroom,
I am in the room behind

your favorite basketball team & all the
statistics that are so important
I am on the other side of the wall
that holds your highschool yearbooks &
the preservation of your precious
freedom

It is dark in here,
But a small light licks
& soothes & melts over the cracks
in the wax. Walls are brittle,
as brittle as orange
falling from my hand
& splintering brighter
across the floor chasing
yellow beams to all corners.

## Change to Blue

Listen, if you dream in blue
I'll be quiet. Nod your head
when you try testing solitude. Later
I will lean myself slightly forward

if you admit
and maybe I will too
that something doubtful lurks
in your collarbones
cold bones
curled in a ball
your back a shield against a chill.

Get over lumps of dreams.
You have to get up in the morning.
Get over bums of dread
always asking for a dollar.
How can you give it to them.
It's the only one you've got.
You've got to admit
you must take care of yourself.

You tell me a soldier walks
across Milwaukee
with a wooden leg.

OK. But if every bus driver in every station
refuses you
an electric blanket of –no not love-
but something dearer, refuses you
a momento from your youth
or your father's youth, refuses you
the rich brown earth
to bury your words in,

then maybe my whisper will go the way
of knobs turning fingers
knobs rattling spare change
knobs falling by the interstate.

Waiting by the curb with a light
until you are inside, the chain
securely fastened, is the easiest
part.

## Flesh Dreams

If the flesh takes needles
bruises easily
without the sting of remorse
that furious unleashing
like a mother's swift & aching guilt
it is because the skin is only resilient
& wants protection.
It is slightly beaten already.
It is tired of keeping up appearances.
It longs.
It wants to be honest.
It spreads itself like a lampshade to be lit.
It wants to know it is alive & it feels.

We could talk of the body
as a kind of battleground, clinically
full of holes & scarred
a big place riddled
with uncertainty, those obvious
and not so obvious
cannonballs that burst without direction.
It leaves the poor sod torn & uneven.
Finally, it gets no memorial plaques, except
strange scenes at night, the face
in the morning not called anything.

There is no chance of a new skin grafting.
What grows back is never smooth & appealing.
You may hope for a kind of bland acceptance.
You may hope for the opiate of a faulty memory
that will leave any ugly moment resting
among many.
A promise is never a medal.   A good bye
can be. We mark ourselves
with prison tattoos

because it does not matter.
We purposely think of that job
we won't get in the future.
& we always laugh cryptically
when thinking of the last laugh.
It will be the only revenge.
The safest things include strange careenings
in the blindness of nights
that are so kind, and talking
thru rushes, bursting
into echo chorus chrome metal door.
At least we can feel this.
It shows we are not totally numb and useless.

## Traveling Nowhere

Watch the sound
against the ribs of these houses
painted and boxlike, in rows and rows
striding along
in soon with a big blue barracuda
barreling along
to flatbeds of casino heaven
but really rusting in a back lot
in Uptown.
That would be your luck trading
sorrows for handshakes
and chances to cross the red line
without silver
without expecting roses

Snows fall on a trip with you
right down to the flesh of Broadway
thighs and red and delight of a shoreline.
It was all about
where even the air bleeds
and cried like two people making it
upstairs or outside a rib joint
It was all about
where there crashes a bottle against brick,
a joke played on morning, the warehouse where
you saw some steps and jumped.

## The First Day

Yes, the look on my face in the mirror
is a road short of desperate, not sure enough
to go out in the morning for milk
or take the bus to a friend's house.
The phone doesn't ring despite the bills
and the downstairs neighbor beats his wife.

I dream of my teeth falling out
by the time I'm thirty.
Huge gaping holes, it worries me,
these scars, these watermarks,
the ruined fabric, these ribbons
from nowhere.
Something smells, the laundry
has been sitting in the kitchen
for a few weeks now.
Can't face the disappearing quarters
and the screaming kids with balloon poodles.
the epics I sat down to discover
weren't there. Only daily trials,
long lines at the bank and unforeseen rules,
trying not to be harsh,
trying to get past the hateful glances
in bus after bus
of loud flashy young mothers
pulling their insolent brood behind them,
and the men
with wall like eyes, grey
and dry, sitting with hands folded
or loosely fluttering, two birds
lost in a train's departing vacuum,
only the windows smooth out in front of them.

## This Poem Makes Me Happy

Because of you
I want to eat bacon
3 times a day, to sit
with my legs
spread, so that I can smell
my own strong self at breakfast
to have secret affairs behind
the world's back, or at least
behind the 7-11, offering
to never look again
in a mirror, but to gaze
at my self constantly, that is
to wonder what it's like
to look through your eyes
Because of you
I want to write good poems
or at least naked ones
big ones that wake me up
in the middle of the night
with a raging hard on
and sour breath that I love
to breathe in so much
and will until you wake up
screaming for air
Or little ones like a probing finger
that, like trust, are too hard to forget
but which can be gently removed
along contours of the spine, fingers
a million blinking eyes rendering infinity
Yes, because of you
I don't mind, not one bit
being pagan, in fact, nuclear
not clear and clearly devastated
Because of you I will never be
happy, and so will write good happy poems

for the rest of my life. And for that
I may even develop the sense of humor
I've always wanted
Because of you I want
to fall down, laughing
get back up, go on
Because of you I will be
relentless, needles of sleep
another soft voice on your answering machine
collection of soft voices, a blue sky forever
sharp as a goodbye, a human interest story
read many times by an old lady
so that she may be
never alone or lonely. Because of you
I will suffer
a rush of lions, a lunch of habits
that have come to feed me
with predictable horrors
words falling from their toothless rotten mouths
me going so far as to say, "Get off of me
No wait, don't get off of me, I need
to be weighed down, or else I will just
float away, just another bum."
Because of you I won't ask
those stupid morning birds to shut up
instead I'll just ignore them, or let you
snore even louder in order to drown
them out, and then I'll pretend
that I will never be robbed
by nazi skinheads ever again
And lastly, because of you
I will never be torn in two, but merely
yeah verily, comfortably, divided
as in half baked, no wait
quiet, raging, quiet, raging, quiet, raging

## Letter to Dawn

shed the remnants of the day
the hard bright sun, the grilling heat
blast of a hell ladened year. It is
summer, my friend, are you surfing
as you read this? I am thinking
about you: off go
my shoes, my shirt,
panties. i've already smoked
some hash, and eaten a big
meal of noodles, raw cucumbers
feta cheese on the side. see, i am
trying to take care of myself.
and get this; when i can remember
i take vitamins in the morning
to ward off the demons
of yeast infections, fleas, garbage
flies, cotchrot, toto. too much
pestilence leads to thoughts
of retribution. too much
of the white stuff and i am really
starting to hear detectives at the door.
funny, when i was a kid it was
angels. so between the falls
i am really trying
to get up consistently and not feel
like shit. 'mortality
is reality. and graveyards
a reminder.' to quote
my own damned self

3:30 this afternoon and it's 100 degrees
plus, and i'm walking around in a black
dress. sweat pours in rivets, riverlets
rivelets. i think of blanche
dubois and other southern fried graces

sure, i'd like a slow gin fizz, right now
no fan is gonna blow
this grit from my skin
no north wind is gonna breeze
in from the cool sea
HOW MUCH HONEY?
one thousand to lick the bottom
of my shoe sucker
the rican boyos in the neighborhood love
the tattoos, something to do with
gangs, prisons, promises
BENITO AND INGLIO, PAPO AND MUERTO
muerto the man with brown bags and
a demon dog with the face of a rat
he did it to himself, in 'college'
as they like to call the penitentiary
with a stereo needle and an electric razor
YOU DON GOTTA LEH DEM TOUCH
        YOUR ARM LIKE DAT
Papo whispers to me JUS TELLEM DATS YORE OLE
        MAN DERE ACROSS DE STREET

now, though, like i said
i've been trying to take care of myself
layin low. 'chillin' as george says.
he's the reason i had to get off the phone
and we weren't doing what my sigh implied; instead
just as i say hello he pulls out
this well over a gram bag singing
no blow no show. suddenly i got the blues
and i can't help my skin
starts to itch and my asshole stricts up
you feel like the bottoms gonna drop out
and you grin seemingly against your will
and you get this urge to fall
to your knees

so we sat on the back porch and listened
to the el and the alley cats, eyes buggin out
drinkin liquids like crazy
he talked about these old blues guys
from the mississippi delta who sold their souls
to the devil to play with all their heart
how do you know, i ask, blasting
IT'S IN THE WORDS he says JUS LISSEN

sometimes i feel
i just gotta jump
i don't like this life right now
i don't like where it's going
because it's going nowhere
all this shuffling from place to place
is pointless, all
this drifting leaves a sticky film
clinging to my memory. i need
to sit and sort out all my lives

this life; cancer of bad memories, want
of revenge, CUT IT OUT, make it clean...

have i complained about the heat and humidity yet?
drains a person, i feel so ill
chewed my lips to pieces yesterday wondering
why i haven't started bleeding yet
only to discover i miscalculated by a week
everything is dream to me i don't punish
my nightmares for being nightmares. i love
them too
(i hear my paranoias before i see them
when i was a kid my dad used to call me
cornhead because i had big ears)

the next probable cause of this everyday
nausea bloat is disease. DISease, rotting female

parts, dave the tattoo man says
DON'T BE SO NEGATIVE
or you'll give yourself tumors
pessimistic or realistic, that is
the question. at least
i'm still walking

because really, the underlying reason for every ache
and pain is not the devil shorn spit of frolicking
on the wrong side, paying for excess thru body
malfunctions but is really the very quickly deteriorating
OZONE LAYER. that's why it's so incredibly hot.
i remember the twilight zone
i've read jg ballard
so can we expect every summer to be as nasty
100 degrees by 10 o'clock
it's the heat that drags you down
sweat drips, it's the cause
of the clogged sinus, the numbed left
big toe, the pinched nerves in my back, the way
my legs feel so heavy sometimes
i'm not so sure
i wanna walk – see, i'm doing alright
with this life, grand in its own way
so that big blue minnesota sky
with a lone kite and the distant rumble
of a young boy's dirtbike
that i keep looking for
on el platforms, walking down milwaukee avenue
always looking for in sunsets, flashing lights
crooked lines, that something
that is always bright, new, inspiring

## Letter to Chris Peditto – September 3, 1987

sept 3 1987


chris p

greetings. this is just a letter to let
you know we're still here. thanks for your
package from last month. just like we've
done on our social calendar august should
be deleted. nothing good has ever happened
to me in august. august has become a month
of dread. the only thing good about august
is that its demise signals the stirrings
of activity. october is the best month.
good things happen in october. i am await-
ing october anxiously. and so on.

i have been reading a lot, trying to fill
the empty space that i'm sure chemicals
are leaving behind. recreational chemicals
that is, not necessarily the evil toxins
breathing city air and eating canned and
processed foods leaves behind. finished
recently the biography of delmore schwartz
which is actually pretty interesting. read
it once before some years ago. my friend
michael hannan picked it up as we were

sitting in the laundry mat and though
normally he is the sort of person who will
read heavy intellectual type stuff he said
this book looked boring. like who cares
about delmore schwartz, echoing what i've
said to him many times about some of the
things he reads. it's actually not boring
at all. then i started man and his symbols
by carl g jung and associates and this book
is pretty fascinating as well.

never did find a job so i will be tutoring
at columbia where i graduated from starting at $7/hr which is a fortune to me. i
think i stand a good chance of tutoring at
roosevelt as well. all starting oct 1. this
is what i actually want to do. much mental
grief could have been spared if i had been
left alone to make use of the last three
months. but NO i succumbed to the pressures
on all sides. ending up extremely nervous
and neurotic and unable to write a word
or concentrate on anything but TV. fuck em
all.

i gather from your letter to brian that
you might not be aware of the fact that
i do have pretty constant contact with
him. in fact we live together and i cook
his dinner every night and wash his dirty
socks. we have a cat named kitty and a
lovely view from our transient hotel
window of the entire chicago skyline. he
works as a furniture mover and is opting
for silence. that's why you haven't heard
from him. one day it will break.

you know, one of the things i liked about

delmore schwartz is the whole idea of it
being necessary to write (and i underline
necessary) because it is the purest way to
KNOW something about an experience. it cap-
tures moments (and i'm not talking kodak
here) it is experience itself. it slows up
time. it is the entire process of thought
captured to its closest proximity. forget
all those negative vibe mongers that want
to convince you that writing is a useless
and pointless activity that leads to nothing. after all, who wants to listen, who
wants to publish your fucken book. so why
bother, right? just a thought.

what's wrong with this picture?

this letter won't be a long one. just wanted to get in touch. i still have the re-
views you sent but don't have the concen-
tration to tell you anything other than i
enjoyed reading them. i didn't think the bc
review was too negative at all, and as far
as the beat review for letter ex the same
is probably the same. it's too long. but i
am in contact with those guys and will be
doing their calendar of events. will make a
copy and pass along.

take care

        Lorri

## Life of the Party

I found myself sinking into the corner of a faded purple sofa. The one tucked back in the farthest corner, in the dimmest light, the one that gave a secluded view of the noisy vibrating loft room. My legs, my mouth and fingers squeezed together in spasms as I fought to keep my eyes from crossing. Blue, green, red and orange-yellow shreds of confetti littered the floor. Streamers of the same day glo hues seemed to sail through the air at regular intervals, accompanied at times by loud hurrahs. Directly in front of me, so directly it was impossible to look around his moving body at the rest of the room, was a thin femmy young man with slicked back pale yellow hair, very neatly dressed in an unwrinkled grey zoot suit. Nothing seemed to bend. His forehead, a pale slab of granite in the moonlight, seemed to blend in with his equally pale hair line so that no distinction could be made between them. It gave his eyebrows a strangely arched look. He danced by himself, content, and the colored confetti fell from his head and shoulders like soft flower petals in a feminine hygiene commercial.

I buried my nose in my styrofoam cup full of foam, overflowing but flat. It dribbled by accident from the corner of my mouth. I chewed my cuticles, shuffled my feet, twisted stiff strands of hair and rolled my eyes. Who did I come with anyway? Leather and Mo sulked by with long black crane legs, huge dark boots, their hands stuffed deep in the pockets of their leathers. Mo had a red bandana around his face and Leather was scowling. They headed for an unoccupied corner where they could sit and sneer, their shoulders swooping concavely forward like black bats. They went by, didn't see me, or were pretending they didn't. I had non-matching prints on tonight.

I glanced around the room, careful not to let my eyes stay in one place too long. Those party people, they were like odd shaped pegs in an idiot savant's gameboard, how he batters them in the wrong hole from time to time, what frustrations, what chuckles. They flocked together in small huddled groups of twos and threes. They leaned, slumped, twisted and sulked, glaring over their shoulders when another peg joined the party, appearing hesitantly at the door, glancing around for a familiar sneer. No one was allowed to smile or laugh or talk about anything but art and haircuts.

A black veil of crepe passed before my foggy eyes. I blinked. The vision exuded a ritual perfume, a catholic incense, in other words, she exuded the smell of a JC Penney teen department. The vision rustled like pigeon wings flapping in a puddle of oily water as she sat down next to me. The seat tilted and I strained to remain upright, to keep from sliding into her, into her dry white skin. The guy following her around with a drink in his hand sat down on the other side of her, pressing a leather covered knee into her black lace stockings. His combat boots were spit polished and the leather barely creased, barely scuffed.

Out of the corner of my eye, I stared at the back of her head. There was a thin straight line perfectly shaved high on the top of her neck, from one ear to the other. It was clipped very short, to the scalp, about her left ear, the other side cascaded in a golden curtain across one lacquered eye, down to her chin. The clasp of the dog collar around her neck intertwined with the black hair. I could see sharp bones jutting out of her back as one shoulder of her sweater careened off, leaving it bare. There were studs about her waist and wrists. Feet were encased in pointy black ankle boots with five inch stiletto heels.

As far as I could tell he had leather pants and a dark overcoat, the kind the Contras wear. Her hair was jet black and sprang from the top of her head like wild asparagus. A gold cross dangled from his left ear and he had mascara and eyeliner drawn carefully around his lashes. The hand clasping the drink was encased in fingerless black leather gloves with large studs around the knuckles. They reeked of musk and Chanel, boy of london and brillo. Combined with the heat and the noise of the room, a previously consumed six pack of black label threatened exploration of a space other than my stomach. I leaned back and belched.

He leaned back and landed big dopey eyes on her face. "Those are marvey earrings and where did you get them? He asked, fondling her earlobes.

She beamed. "Oh these old things. I got them at Chicago reds outlet store, next to Saks, you know the one. These are exact replicas of the Communist Manifesto."

"Oh yes oh yes, they are delicious. And I've been there, such a wonderful place. What a fantastic collection of political coffee table books."

"Oh say, let me tell you you're not kidding around. I pick up all my Mao Tse Tung literature there, not to mention the Worker's party gift certificates."

They paused. He leaned closer, whispering silkenly, "Tell me darling, are you secretly a marxist?"

She smiled coyly, "Oh yes, and a Freudian, aren't you?"

He straightened, "Er, why yes, of course. Wouldn't miss it for the world."

She pouted, looked off into the distance. "I think it's simply dreadful the way these imperialistic pigs have fooled with the rate of income taxes and taken over the function of good clean american fun. It's time for a revolution, don't you agree? Say do you like the Clash?" She fluttered her long black eyelashes.

"Oh they're my fave band. I even slept with Joe once." He stroked her pinkie.

"Oh yeah," she breathed a little closer. "Me too."

"What do you think about all this nuclear business?"

"Oh I'm all for it, honey. It's about time somebody did something, don't you think? I'm an honorary member of Ground Zero and I send regular tax deductible contributions to Doctors With a Cause Anti Nuke Fund. As long as the masses, the poor and underprivileged keep their voice up, eat government cheese and rice, together we can save the world, everyone will have the means to afford to ride in taxis. Get them to write their congressman, boycott the Alpha Romeo dealership down the block, after all it's owned by a sneaky jew, don't you think so, don't you think so?" She peered at him, very serious and solemn. Her wide eyes were misty. "America can be a free and vibrant nation, don't you think so? We must strike at the unwanted elements and discard them, don't you think so?"

He jumped up emphatically. "Oh yes, oh yes, you are such a consciously enlightened woman, a truly beautiful soul." He clasped her hand to his breast.

She gushed. "Well, I have my material instincts to guide me, after all. I have to get involved with real life. Did you attend the May Day Parade last May? No? That's too bad, truly one of the highlights of last season." She placed a soft white hand on his inner thigh. He trembled visibly. "It was so enlightening. And of course the Emma Goldman birthday bash was quite a splash too. Marvey, just marvey."

They paused. he leaned closer. "My dear," he began. "I have something to confess." She leaned her ear forward, eager. "I am also an..." he hesitated. Looked up and around. "I am also an existentialist."

She squealed, "A what? You are?"

He stroked her arm and beamed. "Yes, yes, and a marxist and a liberal democrat. Something's got to be done. Espionage, terrorism, acts of random violence against unwanted elements. I'm all for it."

By now he was pressing himself against her and she was practically leaning backwards into my lap. She groped at him and I got a little irritated. "Say, do you think you two lovebirds could take it somewhere else?"

She turned and glared at me. "Whatsa matter with you? We're having a politically enlightening conversation for your information. Where's your social concern?"

"I lost it in a video production of mall claims court. Why don't you take your politically enlightening conversation into the bathroom, get outta my lap?"

She got a little indignant and puffed out her thin chest in a threat and snarled menacingly. "Watch it, we happen to be anarchists and we don't believe in God."

The smugness on her face was too much. "Oh yeah?" I said. "Well, I'm really and truly the queen of Slam." I stood up, the six pack with me, "and I think you're full of shit and you look like my least favorite geek." I turned to go.

But they had other plans for me. I could tell from the little pink o's formed in the middle of their chins. I saw it coming too late though. Studs landed his favorite studs in my face, slicing my cheek from the corner of my eye to the bridge of my nose. I stepped back in surprise and a warm blob of blood got in my mouth. She tae kwon doed my liver and I sprawled onto my back. Before I could catch my breath, she ground her heel, all five inches, into my eye socket. Through a strange haze I discerned his pulling a small vial from around his neck. He poured the liquid on my face and it began to burn. Through my screams I noted with much relief that the hostess had pulled her M-16 outta the closet to put me outta my misery.

### Editor's Note
*In all likelihood, "Roadsong" has never seen the light of day until now. It was found in a collection of handwritten poems that was presumably meant to be a gift to an aunt and dated 1982. Lorri was 19. In its form and imagery we get to see what will soon be coming with great frequency.*

**Roadsong**
**(for my brothers)**

bought my ticket one way
hopped aboard a speeding bullet
    greyhound bus
now too many cities is a zoo of memories
that could make me like a Saturday sidewalk
  full of X-mas shoppers who don't
  care
 let me tell you brother when you're out there
out there driving into dark night
and city lights in the distance remind you
   of X-mas trees
don't be taken in, don't believe, don't be fooled
it'll pass
it's just another billboard bound city
  stage you're going through

Cafe signs will beckon like a north star
but you won't find a place to sleep
just a one way Texaco gas station
and the Radio on that long stretch of
  highway is just static
with intermittent bursts of farm reports
You'll learn to turn them off

Yes I know you've fallen in love with
   the cities on TV
sparkles lights and glitter nights she's
   like a well paid well laid lady
and you don't see the cracks, you don't
   see the flaws, you don't see the
   human error
but wash that pretty makeup off
her face
   she's just a whore

and you'll be had
I'm afraid for you

but this is your road
and this is your song...

.....I watched in silence
as grey exhaust rose around me –
    he bought his ticket one way.

## Pure

"Let's go to the edge
and look at it."
Fifteen feet down it is dark and thick

If only I could vomit up my heart
Dust it of the white
Blank walls that surround leaving
Grey over streets that yawn
Thick with something escaping
As the rails back up
Yellow nights sauntering to where
I once looked for - - what?
Love?
For beauty and worth?

There was dirt of abandoned floors
The soot of viewless windows
Conveniently blurred
Sprawled across tiles
Still I said
This is the way it is
Must be
Left it at that

Make it something more
I fall into the clean transient promise
Of your arms
tenderly hard X's
For the scratched a white yearning
Make it something more
We're walking the rails to nowhere
It is this:
Into the empty warehouse
of my lips
you come.

## Torch Song
## (In the Shadow of Vesuvius)

Before there were dreams of atomic snowfalls
blackened volcanoes
rose in the distance
in dreams the promise of a river
of red, glacier steampits & bad cowboys
from the corner of the room
scream
Turn on the light and leave it.

Let go of the sky blue
carpet cool as india ink.
Mother reassures me
there are no volcanoes
in North Carolina.
I fall asleep again
and the curtains of her room
gather & quiver with the lick of a flame
The torch of the cannons resume
backfire, roar from a distant
regiment means nothing.
Guided white missiles of flexed
pectoral hamstring keep up.
There's a mutant form of life
on the airwaves tonight.

And so on.
It is a very wan day. The streaks
in the sky are colors of ribbons
of special announcements: deaths
births, other clashes,
tucked away like roses
should be but aren't.
Except for the few times
when the sun stretches

itself out beyond the ribbons
the day remains
limpid
lolling upon itself.
It is a good day for nostalgia,
a different but new burden for the moment.

## Blue Flowers

In his dream he was a woman and his name was Angela, that much he knew and could tell, as he ran quickly down the dim hallway. In a matter of minutes he would realize that he also had a boyfriend by the name of Michael, love of his life, who was on his way over at this very moment Angela ran. So the man Angela found himself running, and he was running to the bathroom. The light was a browning yellow, he noticed absent-ly, like urine stains dried on boxer shorts, he thought as a man. Angela was in a hurry because she was in need of freshening up, since she knew Michael, love of her life, was on his way at this very moment.

As a man, he realized with some vague consternation that he was headed towards the common tenement bathroom in order to scrape the unsightly stubble from his rather rounded shin, and to splash cool cool water on his crotch. It was very hot that day and he knew as Angela that he would smell and be sticky down there. In the bathroom he turned on the water. The ceil-ing, he noticed, was cracked. The yellow brown paint curling off in scrolls, exposing yet another strange hieroglyphic design beneath it. The floor left grit on the bottom of his bare feet. He lifted up his skirt and pulled off his panties. He noticed with some consternation again that they were a little frayed, and that the cotton crotch had little red brown stains on it. He passed the panties, in what he recognized as an unconscious gesture, beneath his nose and pronounced them too rancid to wear. Or rather for Michael, love of his life, to have to peel such a pair to her ankles. If Michael, love of his life, saw those stains he might think the worst. Angela the man threw the soiled panties behind the toilet. Quickly he jumped into the tub, seated his butt on the rim, and grabbed the razor. Gross, it was caked with dull white stuff, and the stainless steel part was rusted. Still, it would have to do. He lathered his stubbled shins with a bar of green soap, and ran the razor over both legs to the knee. Then he lifted his skirt higher as he squatted in the tub and began to splash cool cool water on his naked crotch.

Then the man who was Angela became aware in his dream of a strange crimp in his neck or something, because suddenly his eyes moved and he had a full sight of his naked crotch there between his parted thighs. And he, the man, was truly amazed at the sight of it, how many folds and partings there were. And the color! What color, a deep reddish brown, almost like a crevice of earth. Before he could decide to marvel or be repulsed he felt something moving in those folds, and he craned his neck a little further. Suddenly, a little shiny brown head popped out with a little suction cup noise; my god it was a frog. Incredible. It had jumped out of the man's crotch, and now it squatted on the bottom of the bathtub beneath Angela. He couldn't believe it, couldn't understand it, and he remained squatting and perplexed for a moment, staring at the frog which breathed imperceptively. Then he remembered Michael, love of Angela's life, who was on his way over at that very moment Angela the man squatted there. This was just the sort of thing Michael would not and could not understand. She knew he would cease to love her. He would be totally repulsed. Angela felt the stirring of panic. She tossed the frog onto the broken tiles and forgot about it as she splashed cool cool water on her crotch again and again, trying to rinse herself clean. He just wouldn't understand. She rubbed the green bar of soap desperately in her crack. She was running out of time.

He would be there any moment. Just as she spied the bottle of basin bowl and tile cleaner she heard his heavy footfalls in the hallway. She rinsed desperately. Angela the man was beginning to worry. A frog had jumped out of his cunt. Michael, love of his life, would never love her again if he even so much as suspected. Feeling the floor grit beneath his knees, Angela the man peered through the keyhole. There was Michael, love of his life, in the hall. Yes, he was here. But he was with someone else. A woman in a white sweater. My god, Angela sighed, looking at his crotch again. It looked the same, like deep dark dirt. Angela the man fought from jumping to a dangerous conclusion.

Through the keyhole Angela the man watched the woman in the white sweater as she giggled. Her hair was white as well, and piled high on her head in silvery strands that glinted in the hallway like wire. Her titties stuck way out and were pointed at the ends. Like what? Oh yeah, like torpedoes or little warheads. Michael, love of his life, seemed unconcerned in that yellow brown hallway, leering in the dimness at the white woman's torpedoes. Oh man, thought Angela the man desperately, as he grew suddenly and grippingly paranoid that the door would become transparent, and she would be discovered by the two of them, squatting behind the door with her hands between her legs and shiny brown frogs jumping from her crack.

Through the keyhole Angela the man watched the woman in white turn towards the door, her mouth a red gash in her face, her eyes drawn to bruised proportions. The woman was smiling in a benign way, her lacquered nails digging into the flesh of Michael's back. Michael, love of his life, pinched the tips of the woman's warheads. Angela the man, squatting behind the door that threatened with every passing moment to expose her, knew that the white woman's crack was clean and pink and was quivering now against Michael's thigh as he tweaked those torpedoes. Angela the man felt his own moist crack, and felt despair, felt no love, as the cracked paint from the ceiling rained down onto the broken tiles where she crouched, certain she was part of the door that was no more than a window with a smeared pane of glass, as it was always threatening her with becoming.

## A Modern Story

She set the empty dish down on the coffee table and wiped her greasy lips carefully. She caught her reflection in the mirror and turned to scrutinize her backside; she grimaced with disgust. She decided her thin hair would look better with a little more body so she immediately called the salon and arranged for an appointment for that evening. Over her shoulder she afforded the mirror another glance. As she slumped in the armchair in front of the TV a very favorite song came on the video machine. She jumped up and looked in the mirror again and then back to the images of the handsome boys singing soulfully into the living room and subsequently to her. She sighed dreamily and reached for a tube of lipstick. She lay down again buoyed by the catchy song and forgot momentarily about her broadbackside. She licked her lips. She liked the color on her mouth. It made her feel......special. This is the color those boys would like, she thought. On impulse she went into the bathroom and turned on the faucet. As she leaned over the toilet she pondered over the phallicness of her index finger sliding between her painted lips. When he had finished lunch she wiped off her finger and rinsed her mouth. She looked into the mirror and saw that the lipstick had smeared across her face and down her chin.

## Bad Cup of Coffee

jesusfuckenchrist, it's cafe
bustelo again, generic non
dairy creaming, artificial
sweets then
the phone's dead in your hand
and what was the message
in that song again - -
no benefit, it goes beyond
doubts, the dishes, the dirty
laundry, the refrigerator as it
modulates at midnight, the way
you shave your armpits every night
and put on your best gown
even though you know
he's not there and that cowboy
won't be coming.
                you must
convince yourself
that it has nothing
to do with you, that it was
a wildcat that left
those scratches on his back,
that he hasn't found someone else
to suck his cock each and every morning
before coffee, or that he's really sleeping
with boys again,
because he doesn't need
girls as they are after all
inferior in the brain department, not good
drinking buddies, can't take it
up the ass like a man can.
                    small
hands little mouths, he finds them
worth the car they drive him
around town in, the money they buy him

dinners with, the rent they pay
for the roof over his head,
when he's not out there running
tearing the world down, beating off
on the sights, like a guitar, the red
lights, the way the asphalt
runs on forever,
and if he has to, he'll leave them
an instant polaroid of his prick
on the meat dish and saunter on
while you wait
on a finicky cat, read dreams
about the world, caress the stubble
on your thighs. no, you don't tell yourself
or believe these things
next time you're blowing him in a doorway
and doing all the right stuff
that makes a man a real hero.

## Mad Dog

vomiting in the lap of the holy ghost

I was spreadeagle on the four corners of my bed
the KY jelly & pumice at the ready
to git the Mother of God
who, of course
didn't show up
I'd like to think She was fucking all the dead
of Chernobyl & El Salvador
but She'd have to knock the flies
off Americans
to git that
cock

## Winter: Fifth and Market

### I. Lying in December
                    beneath
the blank
shapeless nod of empty windows
the wino with tombstone
teeth dreams
dry viaducts-
bottomless pools of clear liquid
he gapes
on the sidewalk;
a dead fish

            Coming in
to a vacuum where people
treat their dogs like folks
they know and bless
and guard their precious gold
hours with green plastic credit
                        his coin
rolled on its side, slipped
between the sewer grillings
he barked
"Let this cage collapse
beneath me
so that I might see the City
and live forever"

### II. Fifth and Market
                  corner Henry cries
his morning paper
from dirt pouch to
Kentucky tongue he recalls
a dusk of pure
snowfall lost in a frieightyard

lost on the tracks hollow
with the sad sad bones
of burlingtons

        Against the facade
of yet another brick era
a man with a battered cowboy hat
mumbles about fat ladies
whose imaginations don't allow
their red legs to swell
                he dreams
about the cheekbones of an anonymous Eve
he remembers from a cool and shade lined
youth he insists, "A snake
basking in the sun
won't budge if he is content."


### III. On the Judgment Day the Patrons of William's Food Shop Will Be Ready

                the air beneath
the stained ceiling is sleepy
the ceiling is stained with tobacco spit
the ceiling is sleepy with
the aroma of bacon
grease and eggs and coffee and fried potatoes
                        the transients
of yet another winter
morning remained seated
they never take off their coats
leaning into the refuge
of Henry's morning paper
dawn light loosened the street
a rapid brush glowing through
a smokey window illuminating
all eyes to glass vials
            who's wondering

what would happen
if all the windows
suddenly opened
at the insistence
of the heavy sad rain
outside

## Life of Crime

It's in the difference now
between your clean blonde boyhood
& the dirty grin of an arbitrary convict
who knows shackles & how to break bolts.
I didn't slam a predictable door when I left
& funny how these hooded winking streets
no longer worry me
as their threat becomes my comfort.
& I stumble on
as though any of its ferocious outcomes
the chance of a deserted lot
dirt of doorways
were mere diversions, new challenges
for this new callousness.

Later I will pacify my suspicions
with twenty minutes of quick lust
with that angel convict, some grinning
irish trouble maker.
Then only when caught by the unexpected pang
a letter from home, sudden moment stumble
well i wish I had been born like them
those bad guys, those tough guys, not caring
and oblivious to all categories of pain.
Oh to be able to fall from tall barstools
and get up smirking
or scramble beneath tables
away from bouncers in time
to loud angry music
escaping unscathed and barely embarrassed
is a dumbness that does not bless me.

## Dear John

Respect your nightmares. Breed in their proportions.
It was yellow gravy caring for a classic nausea.
It was raining, an old cliché for living. I got sick
sick, sick, despite the attempted romance of it.
Sick when the moment stuck in my throat, a pastel
color coming on
when I most needed to bleed.
I only wanted it good then.
Clean. Good and clean.

Your refusal was the ease of turning, of choosing
someone else. A real beauty babe
prom queen of an underground scene. yeah
a regular cheerleader. I vote you best couple
to look at. I vote you most likely to succeed.
I vote you Barbie & Ken of the current sub social set.
So good together, all that
beautiful, unscarred flesh, all that california
promise. The two of you could pass
as brother & sister, no hardships there.
They'll be nothing
you won't be able to understand.
There'll be no tough waking
nothing to scar your sleep & trouble you.
There'll be no chance of you hating yourself
four speeds beyond your control.

And if your refusal only leads me to violence
to inner arm bruises & nightcaps upside the head
then let my arm be twisted
& twisted hard enough that the yelling drowns
the inside yelling. I'm craving
a drink of limbs, that twisting intoxication
that might loosen this terrible numbness.
I only wanted good. Good and clean.

Give me a drug quick that will send me
crashing to the floor
in an approximation of living.

Fragment from a Letter to Chris Peditto – May 17, 1987

Hey RE your letter, really. Money talks
but not everyone listens and some of us
don't bother with deodorant at all, prefer-
ring the sweet rancidity of our own bodies.
See, I always get a little dismayed when
anyone talks of 'selling out.' I can
understand wanting recognition and financial
ease as a result of one's efforts, but I
also think there are other ways of
going about it other than joining The Other
Corp(ulentOorate Side, y'know? If you think
the world sucks, and you can put your
fingers on the whys and wherefores, there's
no saving grace in joining that which you
despise - - and what do you mean by 'Popular Culture': Miami Vice calendars? Bruce
Springsteen biographies? The Cosby Kids?
Alexis Carrington maxi pads? MTV? Sid &
Nancy? Of course you mustn't mind me, I've
got a major grudge against the majority of
the world and prefer to stay out of it,
underground and invisible until I can
perfect the means by which I let go
poisonous barbs. See, I'm more interested
in being a thorn in somebody's side than
having a lot of spending cash in my pocket
save for recreational, um, devices....

Poetry doesn't cut it, obviously, which is
something I'm giving alot of thought to.
I won't give it up because it's something I
have a great deal of love for. And in writing poetry I am putting my chaotic universe
into some sort of semblance of order and
beauty. So it is crucial.

## A Prima Donna Poet Replies

to the universal question
posed by those manly editors
of those manly small press publications
that like to print lots of poems
about manly men in bars buying
beer for babes in hopes of getting
laid, "Well I suppose you think
your shit doesn't stink and I bet you are
one of those feminists..."

Oh, contraire
it does stink, in fact
she breathes in every time
a movement is made, alone
in the sanctity of he ablutions
she follows no rules. and that goes for
bed farts, bean tarts, open sewers
raw fields just fertilized
with the waste of humanity
so that bigger things may grow
in fact, when asked
"what do you do?"
she does not reply
"i am a poet"
or
"i teach at a university
while maintaining a small
press publication"
or
"i hate my wife and
screw whores on the side"
or
"i am an alcoholic hoping
to be the next bukowski"
or

"i am a woman who hates men"
or
"i am a writer who likes to write
about the underbelly of a life
i've never actually seen in real life"
oh no, she instead replies
"i am
just offal
in the rectum
of the cosmos
waiting to be shat out." of course
no one believes her
except the editors
of manly small press publications

## Slayer

why does he shake his fist
and grimace like he's jerking off
why does he keep trying
to stick his middle finger in my asshole
why does he spit so thickly
in my mouth that money no longer matters
why does he seed like dragon teeth
until he comes a million warring soldiers
why is his hand on my throat
like the skeletons of past mistakes
why does he bark
until my ears are burdened with lies
why does he shake
until I must deny all my dreams
why am I so alone
when he screams a teeming multitude
why does he wreck the present
just as tomorrow is safely in my hands

## A Hole & A Pulse

"hey mama
wanna coddle my daddy
shake my pissdrop snake
read my lips with your lips
drop my dow jones
push the prize home yeah you look
like a good little horse and buggy
hey baby
wanna suckle on my bottle
bother my drothers
fuck my brother's southern comfort
wanna drum my machine yeah it likes
your rhythm

hey chicita burrito, wanna be my taco
hey looking so fine with me
        can i walk with you
        can i talk with you
        can i spend five of my hard
earned greenbacks on ya baby
                whaddya mean
fuck off
      whaddya mean
five dollars wouldn't buy me
your toe jam to spread on my wonder bread
i worked hard for this five bucks
and it deserves a fuck ya stuck up in the air
like that cuz you're so ugly anyway i
should just waste ya yeah i should rid the
world of some more garbage
i wouldn't let you suck
the dinkleberries from my asshole anyway
you're so ugly so sit on that and screw it
who the hell do you think you are anyway
i outta make you eat my shit yeah
i outta put you in your place yeah"

**Editor's Note**
This is the only scrap known to remain from an exchange of letters between Lorri and Henry Rollins. Lorri opened for a performance of his and Rollins didn't care for her condition or the company she was keeping that night. Rollins being a capital-T Teetotaler and an admitted Type-A personality. This note is a curiosity, to be sure. And all I have is herein contained. We can't tell if there was more to this letter, as it breaks off at the end of the page and no matching continuation could be found. There is no certainty that this particular one was ever sent. But we do know for sure there was more than one exchange of letters between the two.

Unsigned Letter Fragment to Henry Rollins – June 18, 1990

June 18, 1990

Mr. Rollins:

I'm really sorry that you felt my public
exposure at Club Lower Links on June 16,
1990 was such a "piece of shit; even more
so than the last time" ("the last time" I
presume meaning Club Dreamerz on April 22,
1988 where I remember quite clearly - -
because I was so thrilled - - you told me
I was GOOD and that I should WRITE you and
you gave me your address) In any case, so
you have a problem with alcoholics, well
obviously alcoholics have problems too or
else they wouldn't be alcoholics, right?
As it goes, I find this grudge of yours
rather ironic considering some of the
literary influences you've cited IN PRINT - -
Selby, Bukowski, Lenny Bruce (who, by the
way, used to do morphine/cocaine speedballs
before going on stage) - - have all had
chemical dependency problems at one point
or another in their lives. I mean, we all
gotta fight and conquer our demons somehow.
Some of us do and some of us get found blue

in the face and gagged on our own excesses
next to the toilet. regardless, it's not
your place to judge.

But as far as my "piece of shit" goes,
that's part of the point - - TO GET THE
SHIT OUT, coherently, incoherently, whatever it takes not to be a shit, to come to
terms with having been shat on by the true
pieces of shit in this world. Even so, I
consider you still, after all these years
of following your literary aspirations/
endeavors, good and bad, to be an inspi-
ration, and hopefully will maintain the
res(sic) you deserve and will worldwidely
garner as success naturally kneels in your
crusading footsteps. I mean, your
demons have been conquered, I presume,
or you wouldn't have such a heavy hand
towards those that have them rear up life-
long. May the day come - and it will - that
I will have the love of self and self
respect that I won't have to hide behind a
chemical (and I don't always anyway) when
I am standing in front of a room of
strangers spewing forth the intimate
details of my life, the most painful ones,
strangers who would tear me to shreds quite
naturally if I wasn't somehow reaching that
part of     that screams: I AM FUCKED UP
TOO! We all can't be an Uberman like you,
Henry, so try a little compassion - - not
for me because once wounded I don't stick
around for the kill - - but for all those
who have fallen and are looking for the
strength to stand up on their own again.
Those are the kind your literary heroes
write about isn't it?

Letter to Chris Peditto – June 22, 1987


Chris P.

First of all, thanx for your letter and
sorry I haven't responded sooner. I broke
my old typewriter a few weeks ago by throw-
ing it off the table during a drug induced
tantrum. It's an old underwood manual and
I figured it would weather the fall. But I
guess I knocked something crucial loose.
In any case, I've been borrowing this one
which has nicer print, but my friend needed it back for awhile. See, i don't really
like to write letters out by hand anymore
because my handwriting sucks.

Well, enough about typewriters, fer chris-
sakes.

Have you heard of a writer by the name of
Bob Black? he writes mostly criticisms of
existing social structures, right and left,
among other things, has a very interesting way with words.... anyway the reason I
ask is I'm in this correspondence with him
and I got a letter from him just today...
i dunno, it kinda bothered me, because,
while he was chatty and conversational, as

he usually is, he's also, I suspect, what's
commonly known as a dirty old man. (Not
that old mind you. I just mean that
basic prototype) I mean, he's always throw-
ing out these stoopid innuendos (sp?) and
i've always contended that there are more
interesting things in the world to bother
about. Sent me a pic, too, and believe me
honey, ain't even close to being my type.
Now, I'm not going to let it bother me much
because otherwise it's been an interesting exchange of letters so far. It's just,
how do I get this guy to can the bullshit-
- here are some examples: he signs off his
letter with "Tongue in Chick (at Every Opportunity)"; he takes for granted that the
Hannan on the return address is a guy and
is my boyfriend. He writes: If it's OK w/
Hannan or he (?) doesn't need to know, let
me know when you make your tourist pilgrim-
age to Boston. (Am I making too much out of
nothing?); he gave me his phone # (no big
deal, right?); I sent him some poems in-
cluding A Moment of Transcendence, Almost
69 and he made the assumption that the 69
is a reference to the sexual position. (Was
not intentional on my part. several
others I think have taken it to mean that).
So he goes on about this sexual position;
and last of all, which isn't really a
sexual innuendo but is something I'm gonna
blast him for assuming and that is "I
suspect there is a facet of yourself which
might like to be a hippie earth mother"
??!?!?!? I don't remember what I wrote to
give him that idea - - I did write some
about going to the rainbow gathering last
summer and what a bummer of a time I had

- - a hippie earth mother, gimme a fucken
break. Do you remember me from Roea's
wedding a few summers ago? ; well, I was
a sweet young thang compared to the look
on my face these days. you know, you just
get hard, a hard look in your eye after
even just a coupla years of putting yourself to the test.

Anyway, basically I think I'm just getting
something off my chest here. I really do
like writing the guy and this is the first
time I've let stoopid sexist remarks get to
me. I'm not an axe wielding feminist though
I would like a bullet for every man in a
car who has pulled over and assumed I was
for sale. And I think that's the point I'm
trying to avoid. Sex is this thing people
use like a commodity. It's a power play and
I'm a person trying to have a life separate
and pure from all that ugly bullshit. With
the (unintelligible on the copy) fecundity
of flesh available for the right price
today it has more or less rendered the sex
act worthless. My skin is not a thick one;
I just have a certain amount of control
and I give the impression of things bouncing off... what am I talking about anyway? Why this guy bothers me when he writes
sleazy winks my way? My skin is not a thick
one. I can't be touched just anyway and not
suffer(ed) dreadful consequences somewhere
in the recesses... Should I avoid and
ignore his remarks or tell him. Yeah, the
other thing too is this fishing to find out
if I have a main squeeze; that I'll tell
him alright. That this is True Love and I
cannot be swayed. It is my faith. When it's

gone, I'm gone. The matters of the flesh
here are akin to secret ritual which is why
the flesh as a topic is gone on me; like I
said, there are other arenas to use to gain
the acquaintance and respect of someone.

Besides, all my talk about commodities I
will confess to a certain mercenary reason
for wanting to cultivate a respectful working relationship with the writer Bob Black
(notice I said writer, not man) and that
all has to do with the fact he is a
published writer, knows the ins and outs
that I can only speculate at this point
having to do with the wide world of print.
Do you think this is hypocritical or
practical? after all, I'm not trying to
sell myself out so much as creating this
mission to get The Word out of my hands
and into the hearts and souls of, um,
strangers, I guess... Again, what am I
talking about?

Christ, enough of this whining. Sometimes
I think such whining only uncovers me to be
the white uptight bitch I don't think I am.

Two weeks out and I'm still sitting around.
of course last week was unbearably hot; I
am not a hit weather person. Can't stand
to feel heat on my skin, the clamminess of
sweat. Ug. Heat made me sick too so even if
I had a typewriter i probably wouldn't have
done anything. As far as finding a job; I
don't think sitting around and waiting for
something lucrative to pop up in the help
wanted section of the reader is gonna work
so I'm fixing up this resume I did a few

weeks ago and I'm gonna send it out to
all the local book publishing places and
maybe printers, with hope that I'll land
something like a proofreader's job or...
something. What do you think? Do you think
this will work?

I didn't mean to say you had a shit atti-
tude or anything, in my last letter, and I
didn't think you were dumping anything on
me (Hey, so you have to listen to me whine
aimlessly about someone you don't know(?))
I just got this admittedly naive youthful
thing about wanting to stay out of the
system which I know deep down will have
to bend to some compromise. Keep your
values intact. Don't compromise yrself for
The Great God Buck $$$. I dunno. I do think
you're right when you write "Yeah, I wanna
'inform' the popular culture, play a role
in shaping it not relinquishing it to the
ad people and Hollywood executives"

That makes sense. Have you ever read HAS
MODERNISM FAILED by Suzi Gablik? It's
really good. Even though she's mostly talk-
ing about painters she says some very
applicable things about our modern society
in general and how all avant garde move-
ments set out to shock the status quo
conformity scene of the bourgeois middle
class but end up being as you say coopted
and all that rebellious NRG is them
dissipated and rendered harmless and
impotent. Which makes for the 'necessity'
of whatever new avant garde is trying to
make a difference to have to go to more and
more extremes, some of which are just plain

obscene, degrading, and ultimately absorbed
again. Like, what's the point, right? How
much humanity does the individual in the
society have to forfeit by being impli-
cated; here I am thinking of such rumors as
performance artist Chris Burden dying from
a loss of blood after trying to cut off his
dick in a performance, and of some woman,
whose name I just don't know, who hired a
lunatic off the street to rape her for real
for a performance and she was taken away on
an ambulance after her "performance." yes,
the audience I guess just sat through it
and watched. Do you think such a thing made
a difference in their collective lives? Or
do they of course go on as before?

Anyway, only mid afternoon and I'm already
tired. Don't forget BDC's article and one
of these days I will check out HPNews....


                              Lorri

## A moment of Transcendence, Almost 69

dashboard lights gleam UFO
no conversation across the dark
innerstate 80 to detroit iggy
on the tape machine 2 carpenters
from merryville up front my head
asleep in your lap the miles
hum the drone woke me first
then chicago 250 gone then
i blew you good smile
said we survived
the bust
not a thing different
hand tight in my orange hair
your eyes in the passing light
zipper in my mouth
so metallic so secretive
said we'd get there in no time
sooner than expected

> - chicago to nyc
>   sept 86

## The Queen Of Hearts Takes A Big Dump

i dunno what time it is
or if that was you in the truck
or if you're in the bar across the street
payday pushing dollars at the blonde behind the bar
or why this tallbottle in my hand is empty
i'm no woman in the kitchen
no bombshell wet by the fire
waiting to exchange taco tips
and how to keep your man at home mouthmoves

and baby
if i have your baby
i expect ample compensation
and thats more than a dollar a day
to ride the bus with the other mothers one way
and the reminder of how worthless
i can be
after all we could both be packing
some major social diseases
at ease with pariahs
in more ways than one

i predict my heart will go first
before fire, twisted metal.   exploding
satellite debris
maybe by the time i'm in my fading 40's
it flutters alot now
those big shots leave me nullified for days
i cant even talk about it
such a thrill it hurts
but i'll follow what it says
before i resort to any textbook
it all gets burned up anyway
                    - - and the ambiguities
well i don't have to answer to those

## Rat Stories

Number four:

It is a difficult thing to keep from
making fun of those sincere connoisseurs
of words who read with such lovely
afflictations and side of the eye impressions.
Of modern things and divine things
love that is camp when it's not.
The last word always rings in the ear
but the eye is empty: no recipes, no receipts,
no gameplans, no after lunch conclusions,
nothing darling.
It's all icing on the bazooka bubble,
paint that peels off, a can of hairspray
in a queen's bouffant, mere toying
with intention and words that rhyme with tigerlilly.
 Yes, take us away,
take us to the picnic spot that hangs
in an awesomely tidy museum,
where there are no ants and
the food tastes good, no meat, no grease.

Get past this sentence:
I am appalled at the pretense
of poetry, of life in poetry,
of myself...
Who wants to be laughed at
who wants to get caught naked by a stranger.
I have to urgently remind myself
of what ripping away the plastic violets could leave us:
the garbage collectors will quit, move to Florida
we'll choke in our own refuse,
our own blank fear will gape back up at us
a quick decisions tattoo, the name of
a lover we hated, or the mere chance to get caught

in our beginnings.
It is really too much
and classically becomes a choice
between the lesser of two evils. Welcome.

## Flesh in Excess

in a dream venus came
in spurts a bird
in her mouth like a man
squatting silk off bone
crevice pure
the body is a day of ruin
pirate of her dreams
his hand the habit of tender
pawing so round her so helpless
her dancing in a hall of chances
the hour a carcass beneath the table
her haunches the luxurious revolt
his johnny the hard thrust the grinding
right the floor the heavy dope
of obedience
welcome to the vacancy
the better citizen
the honest insult
the fucking difference

**What the Moon Must Think**

i remember the smooth
golden spanish sand
curve of her naked     shoulder
before the light
               fell     down

## How Egyptian Of Me

"We can never really see
ourselves because of the way
our eyes are in our heads.
All we got are mirrors
and other people." Empirically
spoken, a hint for a day passing
windows and other distortions.
Does the singular self deserve such inspections?
Organizations and company trucks to drive me home
that now there must be other things.
Apprehension tattoos my face
A man waiting for the cab insists I have
a piece of jewelry for the rest of my life.
The victim as chimes: who needs that
resurrection of doubt. If a woman says
she is no victim don't argue by pointing
out the semantics of desire.
A fist is no critical theory worthy of such distinctions.
Beneath a bridge I pass out, triangular
silver as silence, a blue without air.
Look at that amazing sky, could I ever be
so innocent again; rustle of leaves
an ocean of distance, sea of regret
in a japanese mouth, riches to wash the asp out
a single penny to derail a slow moving thing.

Drought they say, severe all through
this great midwest. The soil has dried up
refuses bounty, everywhere a desert.
No longer willing to be afraid, I take off
these mirrored shades, start a new life
revive aplomb, saying, so cough us up
these are my bright jars, these are my insides.

## One Death Every Eleven Seconds

When the pillow reaches
around your head in a hammerlock
blue light rings
your eyes with black coal
coal black sadness.
when you're dancing
in one corner of the room
like a little yellow fish
wandering in the wrong skool
the lights are so many
screaming peacocks
eyes its hard to discern the floor
until you hit it.
bouncing off the walls
a silver ball of red magnetic
fields talking slow to the
waitress of the favorite baby girl
who died last week w/out a
murmur overcome, it seems,
by a million emitting machines
all registering "No."

**Still Life (a triangle of sorts)**

The red phone doesn't ring though it aches.
The day is black and swollen.
So is the borrowed room. Everything is
temporary. A siren
is mean and blue. A dog wails for nothing.

The hall is deserted. A man w/ black hair exits
the glass door carrying more than a six pack.
The room wants to crumble, close in
upon itself. It doesn't.
The girl sweeps absently. There is dust
rising from the cracks. She doesn't notice.

He drives the sky
blue convertible
back to his garden. Back to the queen
size bed where his tight wife sleeps
three feet away.
In the morning she won't want
to make love and will
change the sheets again.

## Casual(ity)

afraid to make a scene
to laugh in someone's face
ignorant bystander
even when creeps win out, fart bubbles
in a public pool, or the rumble
of a belch at a family picnic

held my breath underwater once
and nearly died laughing

**My Life As A Big Fat Pig
(in Three Parts)**


**Day One:**

Twenty three is my leanest
Year full of drafty drafts & cold
Spots, sores on open
Windows, no fever in the
Furnace. It is so cold
Up here in this place.

Paint peels from ceiling
Crack. There is rubbish
In every corner. I don't care
I organize my garbage as the wind
Fights to get inside
Hard lefts to the right
This wretched kitchen

Where there is a monster growing
Beneath a pile of ancient moss covered
Dishes: plates, glasses, plastic
Butter bowls, the only fork
in the house. Only the cat knows
Sniffing in places no broom has gone
Before her.
                        Later in the day:
Time moves fast in this day
& age WHAT IS IT?(!) The nuclear Age
The Not Clear age / the ice age, you mean
This Tech No Logical La La Land
of synchronized cumming and/or
hard software (& I don't mean generic-lee
I mean
                        Blah!

Forget it
Bring on the canes & we'll give Every
body a hardy round of whipping posts
& won't that be fun & we'll do it
For profit too.

I am returning for now:
The words I meant to say
something about how everything
is rendered
archaic                because time moves fast now
& it's gone baby
as soon as it's here

Don't count on a man droppin
his kickshift too fast;
let the dust settle on his boots first.


**Day Two:**

P.S.: What is the Nature of Change? (spare change,
cheap change, soft change, quick change, ripe
change, slow change, spare any change at all, sir?)

The most popular form of satisfaction
in this house is
edibly oral
orally edible (that doesn't mean we eat the house
that doesn't mean we eat each other) If only
Ha. but we love to eat food

DREAM: two greasy tostados from Arandas
on Milwaukee & Division, dead of night
where no one but us speaks English
Marc has to recall high school spanish class
Still, it is difficult

to be understood..........end of DREAM
                    if there's not enough $$$$$
then soup
cans of it from the Jewel Store
especially since it's easy to (whisper) steal
& the extra change means cheap beer: Black
Label, Mister Brew, Colt 45 Warheads
        Of course there's always
noodles
Noodles! –what would we do without
Noodles!

Eating seems to be taking the place of
(ssshhh): sex.

Generally speaking food doesn't talk back
You end that argument with a Rolaids
Supposedly canned soup doesn't carry
the current social disease
You don't have to explain yourself to a cheesedog
        an onion bagel loaded w/ cream cheese, or a gallon
        of Neopolitan ice cream
Pizza doesn't make fun of you
French fries don't laugh in your face
Tacos can't tell you what to do
You can't be sexually harassed
        under most circumstances, by a leg
        of fried chicken
A cucumber, bean sprout & mayo sandwich
        on wheat bread does not hiss "Baby baby sweet mama"
        at you when you walk down the street

                            Later in the day:
afternoon aftertaste
mouth is Ugly, Ugly
fig newtons come outta it
therefore it is an instrument

of Uglyness, like
a leather bowler hat, or a ten speed
juicer, or a combustible vacuum creator
or disposable mud pies or a
bronzed bible or even a purple kazoo

Teeth are fungus encased
These fungus Teeth
are just pale gremlins
bad carbons of what I'd really give to you
O, to wake up groanin about fungus Teeth
Whatta wall. It's so hard to talk
when your mouth is full
of Ugly


**Day Three:**

(written when my head was still young:
mortality is reality
graveyard's a reminder
i was thinkin how nice it would be
if someone dedicated their story to me
& maybe i wouldn't be so gone
& maybe i wouldn't be so loose, so lost
lookin for pennies lyin
lincoln side up (that's good luck, ya know)
hello. i miss you
much in the way i miss buses.)

What if everything fell down
and fell down hard, all the walls
of buildings & warehouses
rows & rows of files & files
crashing all around
the banners of their lies and slogans
          useful now only as slingshots

and blankets

The world is sweltering underground
& no one is complaining
Are they used to darkness
to underground crustaceans creeping
across the skin in dreaming
It would be no hardship to walk in silence
to sleep alone, in cold bare rooms
getting used to pain, getting used to fear
getting used to hate
Today is only practice
                                    But later again:
It is really a rare day. It reaches back
to connect certain clear sharp skies, kites on green
hilltops or prairies clasped by yucca
This happens only a moment at a time: is this
eternity—how close are we?

But ha! the poets are really
liars. I know because

the day passes & what battles
begin again
trying to get up
trying not to melt on the subway
The day passes & chases warm spanish mothers
w/ their bundles of darkeyed children
away.

(I don't mean to be a drag)
But it will rain tomorrow. Again.

Ha ha ha ha. The mean ole one eyed dog
He's so mean he has to look at the world
through just one eye and boy (!)
it pisses him off. He'd like nothing more

than to jump that fence & rip my head off. Ha ha ha ha...
He'd like nothing more than to tear my throat
& eat my heart. Ha ha ha ha..ha ha..
Stupid mean ole one eyed dog.

*The Three Graces* by Fred Burkhart
Property of Larry Oberc, used with permission

## 2nd Train Piece

A man has his arm tightly around his woman. She is leaning slightly forward, towards the expanse of the train window. She is watching the edge of the smooth dark rails as they disappear beneath the wheels. It seems they are being swallowed. She is not looking at the man who is staring intently and possessively at her profile. She leans slightly away from his hot breath lying heavy in her tiny ear. He doesn't notice the way the veins curve in the transparency of her pale skin like a miniature muted sea amoeba. He clutches at her tighter and tighter, his hand an iron claw on her arm, until she senses there is no more room to breathe. He presses his bony knee into her thigh like a spear. She leans toward the rails some more and sighs.

## Things To Do When You Have No Home

Be sure to have enough
friends w/ spare sofas
wake up, quietly put on
the same T-shirt
worn 7 days consecutively
and smellin quite like you
creep out into the mornin
the bones in the bottom
of yer feet and knees
are still achin
from walkin the day before
so head to yer fave diner
where a bowl of soup is less
than a dollar
drink 7 cups of coffee
and the mornin is spent
pick up yer bags
and walk slowly
no sense in hurryin now
sit on a bus bench for a while
and talk a long time
about jesus to the woman
next to you
or the black man in the alley
who says he used to play percussion
with the rollin stones
drink beer on a park bench
if someone else buys it
go back to the diner for more coffee
yer calves ache
and yer knees ache
and the small of yer back aches
and yer belly aches
and yer lungs ache
and yer arms ache

and yer heart aches
ride the train to the end
of the line a couple of times
and if you have the money
see a double B feature
and if it's rainin
read a book in the library
it's evenin now
and too cold to sleep in the park
go to a bar
and try to meet a nice man
make sure it's dark enough
he can't tell how shabby yer clothes are
maybe he has his own apartment
and a well stocked refrigerator
and he doesn't have a girlfriend
a sweetheart, a wife
show him yer dimples
even if it hurts
the scars on yer heart
and the bottom of yer feet
when the sun comes up
put on yesterday's T-shirt
worn 8 days consecutively
yer crusty socks and stuffed boots
creep out into the mornin
the bones in the bottom
of yer feet are still achin
a cupa soup is less
than a dollar
write a letter to yer grandma
while yer waitin for the bus
you never get on
tell her yer fine
and not to worry
but don't tell her the worst part
of livin day to day

is not havin a place to cry in privacy
don't tell her the greyhound urinals
suffice for now
don't tell her the bones
in the bottom of yer feet
ache like you were a hundred years old
just tell yer grandma
yer doin fine

Letter to Michael Hathaway – September 29, 1990

29sept90


Michael Hathaway;

Thanks alot for the Books To Colorado
offer; I left town on the 9th tho and
didn't return until just yesterday. Oh
well. I am currently and now concurrently
working on several other collections which
originally were all going into the same
book but now I am beginning to see that
there are several things going on. I sorta
wish I could get someone else interested
in doing one. Any suggestions?

But really, here's what - if you don't mind
me being very personal for a moment. I just
received word that my x-boyfriend died of
a drug overdose and I'm saying this to you
cuz many of the poems I've sent to you he
was in fact the demon behind them, and now
suddenly I realize that there's this body
of work that starts out with me being very
naive and in love and thrilled to death (a
couple of near misses in fact due to the
particular wildness he insisted on) and

then it goes thru hurt and pain and disillusion and there it is. I want to call it Love & Speed after a long poem and... I dunno.

I liked the review very much, of course, since it doesn't say I'm a piece of shit writer and pretentious with all my do-bads and my I'm-so-decadent-and-in-your-face-with-it. Lots O critics like to point this out, I think because they're jealous because of their cushy academic lives and the most decadent they ever get is going to a corner bar and trying to imagine who's a working girl and who's not. OK, sorry, I'm generalizing like crazy. I like the part about being the Janis Joplin of poetry though I'm not planning on biting the dust anytime soon; (this recent death of someone I once loved and who was instrumental in bringing me out of myself has proved what a waste, to go like that, alone and with no faith) Yeah, I thought the review was very cool and accordingly I'm flattered. Ha.....

L

## Borrowed Sleep

From tincans and clanging smooth ice
comes a litany of gas hissing from the corner
from the missile of my forehead, from a horizon of
Can't See Over, from a cacophony of small noises
chirps in brain stew
                          It's a hard
armor we wear waiting for trains
and saviors to happen.
My nightgown reminded you of innocence
once.
You were tempted
once.

Now glades of a city out there, open space
of street and night, the wires
of blue lights winding shadows of dresses
flung back. If only my head
would beat with the drums
of nothing, sigh
with the complaint of a naked bulb
or the lone spinsters fluttering drably
around it
clutching pear breasts in the earth
then I would melt, let go, slip, then come back.

The clock goes round and round tonight.
A barbershop quartet launches gay foreign rounds
of leaving, dear somebody, becoming pieces
of language caught in the throat, slips
over frost on the panes of still life, burning
scraps of definitions in old coats.
I find them everywhere. I wear them out.

The quiet of this hour is too loud, the ticking
of something vanishing and not easy to keep.

It won't be long before I tear again
with teeth that ache
into the heel of your breadline instincts
Protect yourself. I hunger
for warm soup and a blanket for now
that will soften all your hardness.

## Gone/Flesh/Wise

1.
"I wanna be
brain dead," you said, but
only because you love
so much, and that
so much had a habit
of turning against you
Because when you feel
this twisted
you must get as close
to the flesh as possible
maybe even past it
to the bone
This way you can forget
how life is made up
of a series of disappointments
another lying lover
another just missed bus
another clogged toilet

So get drunk, go blind, wail as loud
as the landlord will permit. This is
the only solution
when even the air against your skin
betrays you, being so warm and pure
So throw it up, twist it around
Yes, because this is what you know, this is
what you understand......

2.
The coachhouse windows in back spelled
out the words as though they were
a wish a witch couldn't miss. Creation
is no easy act, tossed off like a spartan
lampooned and fooled by the end. "Her love

festered into hexes." Because I thought
we were special, no matter how awkward
no matter how little there was
to believe in


3.
It was an acid night
I almost gave it up, like
on a silver sarcophagus
a special plate, in a room full
of leopard skins and the black
roses I found out later
you gave to a girl who couldn't
blow you right, so you had to jerk off
on her tits "And they were
ugly anyway" as though
that would make up the difference
O you egyptian fool, I know
how you wanted it, rectum of desire
to push me down, tear me apart
to see me spent like currency so old
it was worthless
I should have shat you out
when I had the chance


4.
reckless and social
there's no place to go
the pang of doubt
that accompanies
every sense of action
rarely occurs
after the moment
it's most likely
to be needed
no wait, what I mean
or what I want

or what we're capable of:
knocking over another beer (empty)
falling into the void/cunt
(another ugly girl); recognizing
the junkies in your new neighborhood - -
o god, and them recognizing you, the shuffle
in your stare, your perpetually pouting mouth;
ignoring the boring poets who refuse to listen
to even the most minuteness, that bone
of a loving gesture long since abandoned
like that stupid girl who just won't let go
of you rising once from between her thighs
is this just an emptiness

5. (The Teacher Said:)
I wanna go like
anger before slaves
the bone of yr past
is not quite insignificant enough

"I'm just a woman
whose guardian angel is raging
who has just stopped
snapping his fingers

6.
there's another world
in the sky tonight
despite odds, I'm vaguely
happy. old flames
simmer to nothing, i'm not
doubting my heart's
absence, nor worried
how shitty this poem is
startled by the revelation
of a young black boy's
curling eyelashes – beautiful

you see, it amazes me
to feel so much sometimes

7.
watching through a tincture
of something unnamable, ah there lies
part of the damage – the first snowfall
knowing purity is now lost
by betrayal
it's not quite despair
it's sharper and meaner than that
I know the look on my face
out in the open now
could flag down a fleet
and you, caught like all the other joes
leave my mouth an empty bracket
to paraphrase your escape: "It was twisted."

8.
the moon
that overwhelming moon
the moodswings of an orphan
the swish of old lady polyester pants
on grace street
meat hook glare of uncaring men
I am overwhelmed
by the moon
by bad moods, thick spittle
on numb lips. o, i know
how eternal of me
to swell with the incidental
like, nothing is suppose to mean anything
like, where there is the spoken truth
there is no betrayal. bumps and grinds
so no body is perfect. and i'm sick enough
to want to get well
I'm not in the mood

for any melody
for some culturally confused mexican
who is newly arrived, listening to the latest
and worst rolling stones record
while coolly (he thinks)
eyeing nuwave girls on belmont
as though a leer was all it took
no, I'm not in the mood for 12 year old boys
who yell at me "arrest him arrest him
arrest him for child molestation!" and then
cackle devilishly, a series of mixed signals
such a mimic of their peers, those bigger boys

9.
I get the feeling sometimes
that I am destined to go
in a freak accident, like maybe
rolling beneath the wheels
of the clark street bus
not singing any lullabies
when it comes to a shuddering halt
lissen: I like to collect dead
flowers, no joke. I have a collection
of them. and i wonder
how many killers does it take to die
and do i have the patience to wait for them
cuz when i say "i just don't know what you mean"
you know i must know damned well

10.
aztec spinning mold
testicled, eventually
you're thinking of a thing
too unnatural to the human race
on the first night of your betrayal
I walk into a scene so full of temptation
I bet you wanna know the details

but the unnamable remains
the most dangerous, like a mute
who refuses to behave like a freak, or a jesus
sore that won't heal. let's just talk
about this year's most popular music
It's safer that way
so what if i like to look
at naked boys and girls
i know what it's like to be
in the throat of it
quick, i know another
dealer, he's got
what we need, weeded and heedful
what we want, get it, false talk
a few sniffles. where do you play
"on the ground, on the ground."

11. GoneFleshWise
because i won't let this moment pass
like all the other ones you let go of
into the nothing of another hour
because i won't let the leer
of a young girl when she first learns
that we all must die
going where no mother can reach you
where there are no angels in the light left always on
it's like this: I don't seriously want to believe
that there are no feasible bridges
that anger is the rule
that we'll always hate ourselves for not being
what we're not in the first place
that sex is no more
than a big babble of wetflesh
and other singularly empty poses
that to be
poked and prodded
is to find reasons to hide

that the skin can't contain worlds
more vast than our daily nakedness
that taking for granted
the space we occupy
is something we all deserve
because sometimes i don't think
that's true, and the hot air
of these words
does not compare
to the growling in my belly
that emits an admittance
of a hunger so deep
you can't give it a name

but what about compassion, you say
beyond where dreams can't wake you
remember: too much of anything
is still a drug
and
under all my mistakes
is a clarity of errors
like not even being remotely
embarrassed to hear
the couple in the next room
fucking, in fact, being
quite intrigued and listening
But get this: it's one thing
to touch yourself and dream
of large translucent flowers
it's another to hear the newscast
of yet another killer of women
who has struck again and
skimming the law of man
will strike again and again

## First Mardi Gras Poem

ah man, new orleans was
bust, was clownbutts
shitting assholes of
great american blubber
was drunken chunks
of crosseyed tourist slobber
in every barrel of brew
in every queen flashing titties
all night long, long past
the one last shot
sticky all through the cheap
bauble thrown streets
while men in secret white sheets
urged your money on into oblivion
like you, with dawn crawling
with garbage and maggotdeath of
dignity, yeah, let's party down
yeah, let's have a good ole time
with men who stumble blind
wearing hats in the shape
of fluorescent rubber condoms
shouting, "I'm just one
of the local dickheads!"
and i believed every word
they guzzled bud belched fast
food creole danced cheap trinkets
forgot history
and the voodoo of beginnings
while we took instant polaroids
like the rest of them, said "Wait
till they see this back home."

## Sunday NYC

The small park garbagemen
have come and gone, sullenly hard
without good warnings; it is to be
expected. They are used to trash
Cops with faces as unmoving as metal
swing their sticks and clock the refuse
of Saturday night. They don't go
for the good morning either.
Is it time to bail out
or what?
I am desperate now, not with
out luck or missing yellow trains
deserted not by lack
of money, a hungry belly, sleeping
in hard random places
            desperate
with the sight of ungainly lovers
one fat, one too thin, faces
pockmarked with small dreams
grown together, We should all be
so not alone, bound
as mirrors, happy
to settle for less than the epic

WANTED: to pass numbly
until this hour is rung again
Bells call good souls to comfort
to such a steadfast, unwrathful pair
of arms, so reliable
The 100th dog pisses by
and by the next tolling
the breakfast specials will be missed

Will I write you?
Always.

## It's Like This Down

-ward motion kinda thing, worse than
top 40 radio on a Saturday afternoon
downtown and try to take some comfort
south in the fact no one knows
where you are. You linger like a smell
of a man whose name you can't remember
                              Or comeon honey
maybe it's just your own clean sweetness
your juice of do-good
Cuz you can make it through any old song
a titty dancer offers you
coke but do you know where
to get – and here her hands jab
in an old routine, tells you everything
you need to know

Spiraling down again, you can't do anything
about a construction worker's dietary
habits, that big arm of meat sitting
next to you in some bar on Wabash; what
a smell, italian beef, anything to get those
juices flowing

Worse still, you can't do anything
about the mutterings of mothers who met
on morning talk shows. Their determined
organization will exclude you every time

So, as soon as you got that figured out
that maybe this building you just jumped from
was maybe the wrong one
then you should be on your way to Mexico
and if not Mexico, then Philadelphia
where from there you can take the locals
through New Jersey. So what

if you got a few infections; it's nothing
a few cool strangers eager to know you
wouldn't care

## The Tall Dream

You can't always see it, but it has the presence of being there. The news of your own self destruction reaches you through ruse. A cat of many colors chases light and then church windows into deep red pulsations of sound and movement. You are in a library of corpuscles, moving cells, in an oriental room of dreams. A bush with large gently flaming flowers nod in a magical mathematical rhythm. It has a silver air of knowing what it is and where it belongs. It is music. It comes from a distant place, where monday morning buses do not roar in the routines of reason. Through triangles of white  light, you see another room, just an ordinary one, where a girl wearing pilot's headphones sits at a table made of yucca. Adjacent to this room green pears and avocados peer from a hidden screen, appear to vibrate. She is listening to these images. Then it all changes as you approach to wonder. A large dead tree stump, its roots twisted beneath the earth, is a wise man before whom pilgrims pause before leaping into the ravine. A punkrock chick kneels in the gutter, a raincoat of plastic garbage bags upon her back. She does not understand yet poverty of spirit. Then there are other creatures, mutants: a big businessman in an impeccable suit of grey lead arrives at the airport. he and his many pieces of feminine luggage are swathed in dull plastic. Voices emanate from an electric heater. It is the language of possibilities. You strain to understand. It is a spoiled young man talking to his first girlfriend long distance. He is threatening her with new conquests and other big breasted women. She must obey him or she will seemingly lose. On the surface of this page swirls many hidden colors, an abundance. Beneath overpasses the innerstate breathes. A dog consumes fiberglass and becomes like us, dirty birds breeding in a dimestore cage. One bird is bare of feathers, is dying. the other birds peck out his eye indifferently. Like a black bead it lays upon the floor. The dying bird does not resist, in fact, huddle closer to the most vicious bird, the one who will deliver the final blow. Are you ready to be shown these words? A nurse will prepare the light, pus on her rubber gloves, a mask upon her light sphincter mouth. Then scissors make words, will be knives in these hands.

## Raw Dog

Caring is drunk
is drank to a close
in a bar between ambition
lost at 5AM, and the second
avenue corner, the all night fruit market
Close out this doorsteps, idols
of maybe tomorrow
where Wednesday truths escape
in the pandemonium of 3 warheads
sweating colorful lies
between propped and casual thighs
Where weekday remains
are relics forged     in a score of pure
adultery     of the PA
chronic stain of night
pit motion found only in us
the hard music

(Routine waits on us with sullenness
spills hot liquid in the lap
when 9AM is not a fact
The feat of the evil eyed arab who sits
endless on the newsstand at second and sixth
he glares from ancient racks: "You no touch
the merchandise. You touch
you buy.")
              So, like, we're still
here to tip the bucket beneath
habitual gloom, the breakfast headlines:
Sleek Commentary     dogs
Professional Concern at 8 12 6 & 10
Trashed with the privates
of the popular apocalypse
fear fissions the young unpaid damage
treads on boots, packages

dread in hearts. Say "We know
all there is to know
about your tidy lies. You deserve us."

Caring is sabotage
is ambushed in the exile
to the unemployed stoop
The bag goes over the head or in it
melted to a necessary salute
a tiny primary to wave, redly
a flag above the flea market
ebb and flow
                    Dying
for a shot, a firing squad of victory
I want something to hold in my arms
a bouquet that wilts on the heart
thrills us as only a trick can
turned on the whole human race
                                        But, hold it
before it all ends
fire on the floor and fading out
in taxi dreams and crashes
vow me
            as a naked escape
would a blockade of grey flannel


                            a morning in the proverbial sense
not the florida postcard
slapping the back in a hard welcome
not the cactus sand in a plastic bag
hung from a rearview mirror
not the number scratched in the dark on flesh
not the clock in the shape of a singular woman
atomically correct
whose tits flash "It's a bargain
it's a bargain." - -
                    OK, make me a strong one

one with a little twist
one that will no longer sob me
the one that won't wake me up cold

## With Love And Speed 1/6/87

### One.

I roll in your crotch sweat
teenage bed, your boy, wanting
my hands to be your hands
ache hard to angry songs
the needle worn
grooves. the diving for blue
or something even greater
than the vast tangle of innerstates
the next billboard rush, the taxi
from Fifth Street
the words that bother, hang out
sick for daze: exit
rails, gone now past future
room and waiting
               Look for me
the valid outlook, OK? The rest
cleave to my teeth, the roof
of a twin story two garage, your mother's
mother's quilt illusions, our impatience
with all shades of beige

The exquisite needn't always be
lovely, diplomatic, knowledged
It can park illegally, buy drugs, blast
eardrums into steady rings mistaken
as a phone at midnight
It can die
or last for two eternal night
It is overheard breathing between sets:
"He would take
to coughing up
demons, carving them
from his heart." It can stare

from eyes totally blown
until the hand must move
in a deliberate gesture: smoothes
hair, closes in on social comment
breaks entry, deflowers, remains alone
but somehow intact


**Two.**

Now, Spanish ladies with hard
hair curlers are casual on a giant train
linking a string of cities stalwart;
I want I want I want
Where am I from?
I come from Chicago      but
before that
"I'm so afraid, I'm so
aflamed." The sheet gets twisted
and my world concern is down for the night
Someone will trigger      laugh
from the backseat of a strange car, groping
big, like the world
or this floor bound mattress
And the lights –
                    Another intersection
   gone
The package is cellophane, complete
A shiny black radiator
and would someone tell him please
I'd follow him anywhere
and that includes thru boot tied nights
on asphalt, with stones beneath the back
and into fire, where the laughing
is terrible and delicious to prove
no such thing as mothers
A man in the room across the crooked hall

coughs and it is not politely: "O Mommy
I'm dying, the room is full
of angels." Hack hack
legs begin slow curl in the air

Everything gets punctured
like rice paper with a nail
Yes, it can be
as Chinese as that, little white
boxes opening in the back
down the avenue of a willing throat
where admit rips the thin material, with love
and speed, as it gathers round
the single chair, the thighs, the windowsill
the frozen outside

## Untitled

...to catch a sleeve on flames
Would it burn my arm
at first
Would it hurt
or feel cool
as dry houses
hands on frozen poles
Would the flame spread
to the wail of red sirens
hoses hissing
the coach house smoldering
smoking
and me, perhaps found
unrecognizable, a little
twisted and curiously
dead.

# Red

one winter love came strange
tapping on cold winter panes moving me to
write red roses after

ms. stein, and indebted
to miss moore, mother of the invisible
dispatch w/ warts

whatta red rose he was
w/ feet like roses, neck like roses, elbow
roses, belly roses

i was a red flannel
gown of naivety; up rise the roses
as deep velvet curtains

no, I did not truly
know roses, as neon swordfish swim away
or darts or feathers or

red mitten lost away
against the white snow; red laughing of candles
red angels in the hall

late in the fall in brown
earth auntie's far flung rose dress steams inside warm
maiden mason jars, safe

in the coldest months, still
sleeping for the thaw. O red was not the quench
of an august noon thirst

red was magnolia lust
dawn panoramas from fire escapes stretching
across water, was not

one show flattened by the
train; tattered dolls rolling in rain gutters
thief sirens cut the same

red as trying to pass
the minutes away – the sum of icicles
goes safe and sweet and numb

where is our amazing
lottery luck, our lanterns, the new chinese
year, the carnival, quick

red left turn on asphalt
hundred miles per hour, clean and forever
washing myself with red

**Untitled 1/6/87**

It's all proportional; if I hit
the same vaults as you did
I would be dead by now, not just
gone but finished.
As it is, I can't believe it
stuck in the very armpit
of the joke
suburbia

**Untitled**

Somewhere there is a balance
Between dirt
& the golden meltdown
(I love; I am dirt)
In symmetry
Tracks come fast and even
Miles beneath the tires
Days pass blessedly / cursed
In oblivion
I remember despite
Memory's fatal black glove
The freight of inebriation
Digging holes for the eclipse
Of a tender moment's annihilation
Dirt to follow, dirt to fall
Golden to long for more

## Untitled Four

you are the taste of a peeled grape
in my mouth and
sips of white champagne to follow course
resulting in
cascades of silver and
pain
spiraling through
the tendons of my back.

you are three mile walks
in the elephantness of 2 am
two old black men argue
and the asphalt is one tear
against their skin
I am destined to walk home alone
shadows that are too thin
still manage to conceal
branches slashing across
in suppressed fury
the plane of my cheek.

you are blood in my eye.

## No Title

rain hangs in fungus pearls
off the black wires
small ugly noisy brown birds
no clouds   just
a grey film hanging over
unrolling   everywhere
the pall of a conquering uniform
the dirge of a filthy marketplace
where goods are for barter
and cheap old souvenirs
leftovers from a family border escape
crystal from someone's broken divorce
one shoe found by the side of a road
and always
old recliners
childhood is no consolation
nor is it an excuse
the yard next door is a muddy swamp
a pool lumped with garbage & cans
odd throwaways
a shark swims by, blue lights flashing
he is our only consolation

## 4.30.90

Unlike the typical stereotype of the depressed women, it does not make me feel better to spend money. Nor can I cure myself by slicing large chunks of flesh from my bones. Or by getting a new haircut or by seeking out an old friend. In fact, these things always make me feel worse, like I've just taken a drug that has made me terribly happy, but now is wearing down quickly.

This week I went into a painting frenzy. Not an artistic one, mind you, but rather I painted everything in the house RED, crimson to be exact, bought at Sears where even President Bush shops for his family at Christmas to insure life remains as homogenized as possible. Chances are though that he didn't venture into the paint section and buy crimson enamel paint like I just did. And so here it goes: the bookshelf, the tv, the rat's cage, the file cabinets, the little basket that holds the scraps of my pathetic mental meanderings ie poems, the basin bowl and tile, the floor, the bathtub, all my boyfriend's drawing utensils, even the kitchen sink. Christ, you'd think a murder was committed in here.

I dunno. Maybe it's the weather changing. They say spring brings round more than flowers in abundance. Maybe it's the little pieces of my womb the ladies at the health clinic keep scraping out for surveillance. Maybe it's that time of the month every day, month in and month out. Maybe I just like the color red (I don't, really). Maybe I'm so fertile and full of blood that it's time to show it.

Even my typewriter is red.

Now, covered with red is not as crazy as it sounds. Remember me when: there were these moods that swooped down with the precision of a guillotine. And there I would be, standing uncomfortably close to myself. rushing and hateful, shooting the blood from a watery grave onto whitewalls of letters I would later mail to "friends."

you see, I'm not crazy. I'm downright healthy.

you dont gotta do nothing, not a thing, just lay there with your hands folded up and rot.

the junkie kid came in about 1155 aprox. It's his eighth overdose this week, wadya think, cant beat 'em away, huh, look at him, he just sits there. WHO'S THAT IN THE CUBICLE NEXT TO HIM. oh that's little billy white, smalltown allstar little league, another relapse of his cancer cells or something, he's really sick, dying in fact. he dont look so good. I'LL SAY. WHO'S THE OLD MAN. oh yeah that's old man weston. WHAT'S HE IN HERE FOR. oh the usual old age, everything's shutting down, you know, all his survivors, the next to the living kin, all bring him in here regularly when another major body organ decides it has had enough and forgets to go on, know what i mean, they all keep insisting that we hook him up to whatever major medical science breakthru gadget they saw on entertainment last night, hell, their insurance'll cover the cost of squeezing one more breath outa the old guy, anything to keep him going a little while longer so they can settle back with the kickback and not feel guilty about a damned thing, yeah, whatever. AND, SO, WHAT'S THE JUNKIE KID'S STORY. ah, i think his parents wouldn't let him have the car last night. ha ha well you know why not. hey listen, he's talking to the little freak with cancer, the cancer freak, what's he saying. NOW WHY DO YOU CALL THE POOR KID A FREAK, HE CAN'T HELP IT HE GOT A DISEASE THET TRANSFORMS HIM. look at the kid willya, he aint got no hair cause it's all fallen out from the radiation treatments the men in white robes make him undergo every other day, his skin is green, his eyes look like they got lost somewhere in a cave where there aint no light, and his teeth, why his teeth are about as bad as the junkie kid's and how much is that sayin, huh, what's he saying that junkie kid.

you got it made asshole, dont you realize how easy it is to be dead pal, allya gotta do is lay there, see, ya dont gotta do nothing for nobody, dont gotta talk to your mother, dont gotta go get a job, don't gotta do nothing.

and the junkie kid smiled at the little cancer freak, the cancerous kid, and reached out and poked a pale arm, and the cancerous kid just stared at him with moon eyes cuz he cant talk cuz he's got tubes in his mouth and tubes in his nose and tubes on either side of his head, he can barely gulp, and he stared at the junkie kid, at his greasy hair and his greasy hospital pajamas and his greasy skin and when the junkie kid grinned the cancerous kid could see where his teeth were starting to rot. then the cancerous kid thought about the raffle he entered, a special raffle, Magic Trips for Kids Who are Dying of Terminal Diseases. if he won he would get to go anywhere he wants before he kicks off. he'd get a last shot at something.

*    *    *    *

look son you can't go around in circles all your life. you have to stop one day to bake the roses. the way you live your life now in such a tailspin, why it's pure indulgence. surely you got more to do than creep around your house half asleep, like a zombie, smoking too many cigarettes and drinking and god knows what else, son, look, listen, whadya gonna do when me and ma kick off, huh, you wanna good old age dontcha, wanna place to live that you dont gotta leave, dontcha, you wanna spend your last days in the sun dontcha.

End of Part Seven

## Three Sonnets

I.
To lounge on a summer swing is the reason to call
But the cause is the young man himself
Or maybe it's just that ugly red scar
Running the length from wrist to crease
Across the hallvein that carries repetitions
Of 17byears for 2 ugly inches
As testimony that a knife, 2 quarts of cheap vodka
A fistful of Valium could not kill him   But what
About adult numbness   He reminds you
Of your own dark room and a hangover dream
In the bathrooms of 17 years lost and
Dreary stations vomiting up hearts and
Cracker mirrors because your mama could not
Love you

II.
Turn pain into Art - - it is vain, it does not make
Sense murmured into the mouthpiece
But this is the knife, the doctor's incision
The one second alarm before timebomb results
Brakes regained before mid cliff flight
The distressed mystery woman helicoptered away
Pain into Art is the jungle
Machete that weeps red tears but saves
You in the end anyway
Needless to say he didn't believe me
And pain is nothing more than hate
And in art he would kill her, the girl
Who fucked him over once & dumped him again
Young in the pit of his own dungeon heart

III.
His front porch is grey green and shiny
Covered with October and a creaking
Scent of November   2 larger than life
Oak trees bleed in naked black arches
Against afternoon blue across rainwater eaves
It is only twenty minutes
From shackled crumpling backsteps, hidden sores
Of accordion city days, from the old story of closet
Upon closet hole home to this Saturday afternoon
In this sun I will dare to breathe
And breathe hard again   And roll my old clothes
In the burning red earth & laugh & laugh
And he will laugh with me and understand
The strands of grey in my hair and trust me

## The Limbo Express

"I got the fear!" Just as Father William predicted, paid in Pompeii, a pie in the face, the predilection toward self injection, laid to reject, insecticide, a whole pile of cows. "I got the fear!" O man o man o man, do I have it; that flapping of black in the corners of my eyes when I'm just trying to get clean; the sleep that keeps me up, huddled in the tub wishing the waters would stay hot; watching the room for any sign that this ringing in my ears is not really death peeling garlic in the kitchen. It's so cold up here in this place. I wave my hands on either side of my face to show him what I really mean. I stomp my boots cuz you know what it's like not to think. You might know what I mean when I say I get nervous

cuz I get to sink into the words as they are to me: sounding off. No name droppings allowed in here. I keep a clean house. My head threatens me with extinction. How about this dandy lion: "Lorri had a baby and her head popped off!" So. Here. Headless babies. Blue air. Green grass. Two black birds circle in the sky slowly, cry like distance ringing. I am riding down a big hill on my bicycle as fast as I can go. The screw holding the front wheels slips away and the tire parts jagged company. Flipped over the handle bars, full speed ahead. I land hard and flat. All the air is sucked with this simple cessation of momentum. Eyes open, there is only that huge blue sky. Her hugeness. To call my mother's name I am so scared! But all that comes out is a strangle of sound. Blue air. Green grass,. two black birds circle in the air slowly, cry like distance ringing. I wait for the fear to subside so I can breathe again.

he thinks he is so strong i wanna crush him i know the extent of his fear

THE POET RECREATES HER SELF BY FALLING/ IN
LOVE/ IT IS NOT THE OBJECT/ OF THE FALL/ BUT
THE FALL ITSELF/ IS IT/ THE BIRTH/

whore: one regarded as actuated by corrupt, unworthy, or
idolatrous motives

Jack mumbled slowly as he choked to death on his own blood.
"You must write to live, you must live to write." "But Jack," I
countered, holding him upright to postpone
a little while longer the end of his life, so that I might write
down the most memorable of the last of his words correctly for
my master thesis. "But Jack, I don't
understand. What do you mean live to write, write to live?"
"That's what it is! That's what it is!" He tried to scream at me
and konk me over the head with a cheap wine
bottle, but he missed. His mouth was full of gangrenous vomit.
he stank like piss. He was choking on the sum of his own excesses. he made me sick. But I had to keep him alive a little
longer. I had to know! "Jack, do you think I should go to grad
school?" I was really shaking him now. How inconsiderate
writers were, really, ultimately. All they cared about were their
own sodden lives. How ever would I finish this interview? the
dead weight in my arms was enough. "Well," I thought, "maybe
I can back up what I mean with pointless abstract theories."
Emboldened by this I left Jack
stewing in his own waste. I didn't need him anymore. I was
a modern writer. What I had never experienced I could just
make up. Or steal from other writers. Or even
history.

whoring: to pursue a faithless, unworthy, or idolatrous
desire

YOU HAVE BEEN requested not to look at the present moment
in terms of what has come before it. Nothing will be allowed
to follow. "What is this?" I snap the information impatiently.
It goes. He says: "All women are whores by the time they get

to me because of the way they've been dicked around by other men in their pasts. They automatically assume that i will do the same. And so that is what they expect.

So by the time I get to them they have become very mercenary and have relationships based on what they can get out of a man." He raises his fist as though he is going to punch me. He is 5'2 and I have at least 20 pounds on him. "There ain't nuthin wrong with me there ain't nuthin wrong with me! Do you hear me!" he's

pouting. Should I tell him now what whores writers are or should I wait until he starts calling me mother. "Stop shouting at me." I say. He accuses me of

 believing I'm special. "Well at least I believe." I counter. This throws him into another fever. What's with these male juvenile delinquent types. They really start

raging when some femme thing gets the better of them. Wonder how they've managed to proliferate.


"You have neither the face nor the body nor the brains to make it in this world." This is when the slasher film starts. I pinch myself. "I'm here now, ain't I."


REPEAT "You have neither the face nor the body nor the brains to make it in this world." I draw foreign vistas on scraps of paper I find in the street. A mountain of a

man sprawls on the sidewalk, his rags fallen around his swollen feet. You can see the dirt in the crack of his ass. His hand reaches up beseechingly. His skin is caked with filth and the air around him is fetid with his stench, so much so that I must laugh as I pass him, at the assault on my nose, at the way I naturally recoil from the sight of his bare buttocks.


REPEAT "You have neither the face nor the body nor the brains to make it in this world." Using the knife he gave me to protect myself with, I attempt to cut open a

large vein in my arm. i want to see how it naturally dodges my attack, feinting first right and then left, and then collapsing for good. Look, you can't hurt me. Give me a black eye, and I will give myself two. Wave that knife like a hero in my face, and I will take it from you and stick it in my heart. Drag me across this synthetic  rug so that I sustain minor rug burns, and I will pour gasoline in my hair and set it aflame.

REPEAT "You have neither the face nor the body nor the brains to make it in this world." Listen, I'm tired of repetition and a whole world caught up in routine and a
thousand other pointless circles. Wait until you discover what a whore a writer is. I'll suck the words right out of your mouth. I'll take your life and twist it in ways you
never imagined, not in your wildest excuse for a dream. "Ah, yes. I'll have two of the cruelest things you can do..."

idolatry: the worship of a physical object as a god; immoderate in attachment or devotion to something

TRAILS Some experience is difficult to translate. Language of air. Meaning dissipates. Pillar and breast the beast eats the poppy, dies of love. Desire: why erect this phalanx of smooth moves, the codes of social being... trees gorge themselves, knotted by the pressure of the rocks. the pleasure of the fuck is movement and sound as it becomes the measure by which all other things flounder. Misery loves company, will settle for a one night stand.

REPEAT "I create myself from out of the ashes. Each time I am torn down, ripped out of the sky, bombed out of my mind, I return bigger and stronger. Soon, I will no longer be possessed by the need to be destroyed.

## Over And Over Again Like A Tattoo

Knot for the gist or the jugular
in a singular chop chop
No applause, here quick
Take two of these tick released dreams
Then apply the balm of a bomb
Across the void of a voice
If pain persists
So much for glamour and grammar
Where nothing resists
In the everglades of truth
Where the evangelist has you
On the examination table, has you
Turked in this world. "The art
Of the rats
Was that
They ate too much, for the city
was made of trash, refuse
Of all colors and sizes."
During the fall
You had to live
Like a slaughter
Or you would have been
Yourself
The rasping laugh, the one hand clap
You wreck sex the annotated ritual
You jerk it like it would save you
Undressed in Saturday blondes
You succumb sucking
To that easy spike temptation
So hard and so often
It builds you, keeps you up there

# Sex Mad

I had an appointment at the gynecological office. As I entered I was taken by the fact it looked just like the inside of a comfortable commuter train. Replete with reclining sofas and soft pastel paddings for the stirrups. I was early so I was told to wait and was given two small rubber caps to contemplate. They told me these would be placed over my cervix and then the procedure would be finished. the rubber nipples were bright green and came in a handy carrying case much like what contact lenses are carried in. Since I had some extra time I decided to go for a walk. the offices were located in very beautiful surroundings near a man made river with lovely carefully groomed foliage on its banks. I strolled down the sidewalk along that lovely man made river. the grass was green, the sky was blue and cloudless. I carried the little rubber caps in my pocket and took them out to admire them from time to time.

I came to a bustop. And I saw my brother! He was running for the bus and he was a small child again going to school. He was dressed in some kind of super hero outfit and if he didn't hurry it was clear he would miss his bus. And there, he missed it! I watched him leap into the air and grab onto a sign advertising toothpaste that was pasted on the side of the bus. I thought once again, as I often think of my brother, what a clever fella.

I'm not sure what happened to me but I must have run after the bus because suddenly I was very far away from the gynecological office and my appointment to have those bright green rubber nipples inserted over my cervix was coming up soon. I began to run back in a slow but steady jog. As I passed this house I happened to look up and I noticed a mediterranean man sitting in the balcony with his answering machine. I heard a message and somehow knew it was from his wife. She said, "Darling, am here with a man much better than you. He is very handsome and he has a very large penis. We are going to have mad passionate sex." Then she hung up. The husband was fuming.

Before long I met the wife and her lover, and they invited me back to her husband's house. I don't know why I decided to go when I had this appointment at the gynecologist. Maybe it was her wild gypsy looks. The wife not only decided that I would join their mad sex fun, but she had also magically endowed her lover – with a cock the size of a horse's. I'm not kidding. It was so large I could barely get my fist around it let alone in my mouth. The wife decided we would have our fun out on the balcony. The husband stayed in some other room, his presence a sulk in our midst.

In the balcony we were all naked and the wife decided she wanted that cock that was the size of a horse's up her ass and so with her wild variety of dildos it became my position to fluff her. The first one was purple and it slid in easily. And I worked at the same time with my other hand on her clit, going around in circles. She was very excited. She was squirming like mad. And I whispered in her ear those things I would do to her if only I had more than one hand on her purple dildo and the other swallowed  by her upper thighs. This made her squirm like mad even more, and moan, and buck.

Then she said she was ready for her horse man. But too bad. Not all magic spells are the best ones. Not with all the lubricant in the house was she able to gracefully take it.

So instead she gave me a vibrating device and showed me where to put it. With the other hand I was commanded to grab horse-man. I showed them mine but they could care less. They didn't even see me. They were moaning with their eyes shut. I rubbed myself against a corner of a table and didn't say anything.

Later, there were others. Four or five men sitting around in front of the television. I am dressed but I am attempting to un-dress one of them, a young blonde haired man in a flannel shirt, jeans, and baseball cap. I am so hot and so ready from having had to fluff the gypsy woman and her stupid horselover that it hasn't occurred to me that the scene has changed. That I am no longer with the wife and her lover but in this living room. They are watching TV and drinking cheap beer. I am trying to undress one of them and he is ignoring me though I do manage to get all his clothes off. No one notices. And I think to myself, he belongs to me. He just sits there and laughs, naked with his friends who don't notice this. By now I am rubbing myself so hard it hurts. And worse yet, I am fully clothed.

A program comes on the TV that commands their entire attention. It is about women who have shaved their pussies. Completely. Naked. Shorn of locks. I exclaim, hey, whaddo you know. Mine is shaved! But the men haven't heard. They're saying Oh Yuck. Gross. If My Sister Or My Mother Ever Did That I'd Have To Kill Her That's So Gross. What Kind Of Woman Would Do Such A Thing To Herself Gross Ooo Grody. And they all slap each others' right hand with their secret special handshake and take long drags on their beers which are all backwash by now. And another show comes on the toob and this one is about a very tall bald headed man from Australia who is attempting to save the world from impending ecological nuclear doom thru top 40 music. He is a national hero. He shaves his head every day to avoid unsightly stubble. To help pay for his campaign he does commercials for razors. The boys all think he's really cool and they buy his records and listen to his speeches. He's trying to save the world.

## Left Bank

It should have been a warning: the perfume the key
Yet I dared to breathe again. A woman walked
Through the train I was gone.
                                    I am left
asking: how far away have I come
From the firmness of legs crossing tracks
Splintering on the skin. Round belly
Of my mother, mother me. You speak of homes
I am homeless
For breasts that rise on the earth like
The hills of northern Italy
Where ships fly & lonely broken castles nod
In the spindle spin mist; intruders in a care less age.

The doors close & the southern summer morning
Is hidden in the crevice
Of your pale magnolia arm
In the brilliance of outdoor tables & accordion monkeys
In the unfolding of yourself
Over the expansiveness of an afternoon
Cheekbones so golden they were knives – O I wish
You were here to cut me now.

I am a stone falling from the empty guard tower
I am my own barbed wire; i coiled around you once
I would coil around you again
If only for the time it takes
To leave this train. We escape
But we come back
One tiny drop of scented oil on heated flesh
Tattooed me forever. The train stops here.
Good bye again.

## Small

hands little mouths, he finds them
worth the car they drive him around
town with, the money they buy him
dinners with, the rent they pay
for this weeks' roof over his head
when he's not out there running
tearing the world down, beating off
on the sights, the red lights, the way
the asphalt runs on forever
and if he has to he'll leave them
an instant polaroid of his prick
on the meatdish, and saunter on
while you wait
accept collect phone calls
read dreams about the world, caress
the stubble on your thighs. no, don't
tell yourself or believe these things
next time you're blowing him in a doorway
and doing all the right stuff
that makes a real man a hero

## Saturday Almost Sunday

lingering in the detroit cold
hidden habit of your face
I am stranded
at the kitchen table
the shoulder where the orange fires
the deep cut on my hand
burn

scattered
with all the harsh slang
stealing before us
choked on the happy banner
that tore across the august sky
it isn't enough to want
to be part of something larger
race to the end result
the lid on the door you would jump from
like all the other joes
who have set fire
to the clock on the floor

wound each night with a knife
it stops two minutes grinding
blue before the word love
minor as a soundtrack
somebody's favorite deathwish
the difference beneath your sleeve
or the world
in the crook of your arm
"When you're broke
you're alive in a new way."

**New Reasons For Nausea**

A man has his eyes screwed shut
with barbed wire
Long black trains hiss through the valley
of his lips

The confused man's brain exits the panels
in the back of his head
He falls then to the muddy streets
paved with the glitter of rain &
the footsteps of unladened donkeys

Dead he is a heavy man.


(to be continued)

## July in Chicago

downtown pigeons peck at dirty
bits on the roof of the ymca
on chicago & state
where i live
in so much uncertainty
now in the clinging heat
of a downhill july
after having jumped
the sinking cardboard boat
of love & frustration
from a man
only a man, twisted
w/ his fear & helplessness
it is easy to throw down
what you cannot possess; target
of flesh, my lips still
bare the scars of splits
direct hits
and so i land
in this place of tired history
where i meet old tumors
ready to pass the buck
who talk of cafeterias
filled in the early mornings
w/ the relief of junkies
who have made it through again
of corner rooms, shooting
speed, of blackouts
that wake a man up
on the 20th floor, his fingers around
a black whore's throat
as she gags
as he tries to hit her
in the jugular, the only place left
not hard and impenetrable

## After Midnight in October

Latenight no relics
To make connections, maintain
You would have called by now
Later there'll be paybacks
Bad poems that diffuse the bulb
Of getting up in the morning
No More museums; they remind us
Of the dead
Give us essays on essence
How to get up
Night tribes beat on through
Endless empty, such voodoo
After midnight in October can't rest
Can't resist can't get away from myself
Long enough to catch the B train
News is silent, stopped foiled again
By rain, by reunions, debts and rebellion
Fear of a room that won't be mine
Build the slow rise to midnight
Fall orange to the floor
Morning the light
The ambush the hearse
Hurts my eyes
Please turn it off
Leave it

# And The Corpse Had Numerous Tattoos

translate   transform   transcend

as his mouth became a huge gaping cavern making to swallow me whole, i flashed back to the man who rendered me first. french kissed. he was a big red haired soldier from alabama. he was missing his front teeth. i remember... i was fourteen, fat, with braces. we were sitting in an empty room, berlin stretched out before us, light filtering in the way that only light can filter. he stuck his tongue in my mouth. i thrilled to it. jerked away later only because of the way soldiers talk to one another, in other words, my dad found out, he hit me. he was so pissed that his oldest daughter would let a soldier kiss her and become the talk of the barracks with her wanton ways. but i was fourteen, fat, with braces... my best friend Yolanda, who was this luscious puerto rican girl, she said i was lucky he even looked at me, let alone stick his tongue in my mouth thru the gap in his teeth... now, in the present, i know enough to say "No" and i roll from beneath this big man. there's no point in giving myself away anymore. "look" i tell him "this isn't fair to your girlfriend, you know. she has feelings too." i am a guest on their floor, a stranger in their city. the minute she leaves for her job at a vetenarian office, he lays down on top of me. yesterday morning I let him. he's an old friend. this morning it doesn't make a difference, not at all.


MEMORY

It was almost midnight when the man heard the ruckus in the alley. In this neighborhood it could mean any form of do-bad. He went out on his back porch when he heard a girl screaming. Squinting into dark shadows by the dumpsters he saw this big guy. He was holding a squirming girl by the neck face down in the dirt. She was beating the ground with her fists and yelling. The man on the porch was alarmed for her and yelled something. The sound startled the big guy and he lumbered upward, a scary monster of a man, a stupid animal, a big foot man. It must have been the opportunity the girl needed because she scampered to her feet and ran away. The big guy just stood there, a blank stupid look on his face...

(Memory, as she blasts yet another shot of cocaine: "I used to have this lover. Smooth injection; he couldn't say no to the powders. They had this power over him. One night we were storming around and we end up at this place called the rainbow. Dry mouth, the jitters hit him quick; i was an instant suspicion. The thing was, was I was run down with The Need too. I felt so ashamed. We ended up in this alley and I somehow managed to wrestle the rig from his hand. Next thing I know he's got me down in the dirt I'm screaming my fucken head off. A light comes on somewhere and like a bad monster he's startled, lumbers. I make my getaway. Locking myself in the john of the bar, I drive in that useless point again and again, never getting enough of a rush, left hopeless, without a home. Stupid with the big scatters. So deliberately desperate. After all, we did this to ourselves, we did it, I'm telling you. We did it to ourselves, like, on purpose, but which purpose? If it's worth crawling on the ground distrusting someone you thought you loved... He fixed dose after dose in the darkness of the alley behind a garbage dumpster, does that seem appropriate? He could hardly speak he was wired he was so electrified he was frying. Can you hear what I'm saying. It's all chemical lies. Standing in that black backwater alley looking for pigs and thinking, trying to talk myself into believing I was doing something so graceful cuz it was all so contrary to all that screams at you to LIVE. My eyes long for light, and what do I do – I shoot myself up in the dark, I am wed to death then as though it were just another black pinwheeling blast turning my eyes inward to silver, ring ring, the fucken phone is off the hook again.

POEM (strong radiance)

I was in the heaviest of cities, the city of my dreams
time
the inertia of the world
the death of memory

STINK your name is wood in my mouth, silence
the color verbatim, rimmed now, the flag is ready
to rag out the hour
cobra world
the posse wants the privilege
the religion to track down any woman
who persists in strong radiance
that smooth seepage from lung to lung
long after the source of excitation
has begun and gone....


VENUS

It all started with a chemical mishap. The heavy set man on
Wood Street, dressed in camouflage, saw my desperation first.
He moved in for the easy mark. He flicked his glance over me
like a viper tongue. Started talking real quick into my need. But
she said, that big puerto rican girl who came sliding smooth
out the shadows, "Watch him baby, he burns, yes, he burns."
And I followed her. She said her name was Venus and I asked
her, "Is that your real name?" And she answered, "It's the name
my mother gave me." And I asked her, "Do you know who
Venus is?" And she answered "Yes she is the goddess of love.
She habitually stood on the corner of Ashland, Milwaukee, &
Division after parking her battered station wagon in the Zayre
parking lot. After copping a rock Venus led me across the street
to a basement off an alley where in a room seven others waited
for her to return. They had the look of devastated children...
how can I explain the look of wonder the woman gave me, as

though I were a light that had wandered in... I stumbled, unable to see through the darkness. Venus showed me her collection of dog bites. I must have looked mute, for communication is laceration, anguish a serpent, the mother of temptation. I was perfectly ready for the score. She asked that I not get off in front of the others, for my method of injection would disturb them. Though I did not fully understand this, I complied and turned around to face the room she indicated. And the room was only a hole in the earth. The concrete walls had collapsed in here. As I held out my arm rigid and looked for a vein in a spear of light that came weakly over my shoulder I heard the scurrying of small rodent feet, christ, as mute as the apocalypse...

## TAKE A VACATION FROM YOUR BODY

She goes to the Art Institute. He sells real estate. This year they're really into spending their money on heroin, that very stepped upon white trash sold by knowing jokers who hang out in the park after dark and wait for dumb white kids to show up with their large bills. I run into The Couple of the Year at the Rainbow Club. It's her birthday and they're, you know, celebrating. For some reason she's so very happy to see me. After a brief conference between the two of them, she tells me I get to be her birthday present tonight. Hmm, how bout that. It doesn't seem like such a bad idea. Back at this very nice and spacious loft, parked in a part of town I don't recall having ever been to before, we three get off. I, of course, going last and getting the smallest blast, but that's OK because you know beggars can't be beggars, they have to sit and appreciate anything you throw them. So, it's all OK, and this white dope makes him a little, uh, impotent which can be an OK thing if you're a woman who likes women and don't need the male member to interfere right off the bat. But no, instead she manages very well, compensates for him with an 11 inch hunk of molded latex. Which I guess is OK. It makes her happy and I wonder what else they use it for. Naked later in the shower he further compensates for his lack thereof by taking pictures, the likes of which, by the way, I have yet to gaze upon, not really being too curious to see pictures of myself extremely fucked up and naked in a shower with a woman just as slit eyed as myself. At some point he manages to rouse himself and there the fun begins. I guess. Later they disappear into the bathroom together I assume to hit themselves again and not wanting to get TOO involved with me, save this special moment for themselves. When they come back to bed she whispers to me, "He's feeling a little insecure, do you mind if I take you home now?" And here I am, naked and warm in a nice comfortable bed sandwiched between two perfectly nice bodies and so I reply "No, I think I'll stay here thank you" and it was actually pretty easy to convince the man that he was Perfect, O daddio, my intentions are all mine once again, just as the image of what I wanted becomes what I have now; I slept on, waking out of dreams of black velvet curtains to hear them grunting in fucking unison. And then later, in the morning, as she's very kindly driving me home, that bright flash of daytime sunlight was such that I vomited all over the front seat of her car. Kindly, she asked, "Are you OK honey?" To which I reply, "Uhhh..."


INTERNAL COMBUSTION

I'm doing that internal combustion thing again, where burn spots suddenly appear on my skin, where I burn for hours, with no recollection of having touched anything hot. Some would say Anxiety but it's not as beat as that ; you know the curious mixture of elation and dread; emotional speedballs, yes? I finally gave up one day and took myself downtown to some mental health clinic emergency. I left my job and walked right on in and said the only thing left in my brain which was "I'm fucked." And I showed them everything, those bright earnest faces you could tell had a future in front of them. And I showed them the insides of my arms, the bruises, and for three hours a number of nice faces asked me questions in such a soothing way that I answered all of them without lying or exaggerating. And I felt better, yes, I almost felt good, like I had done something right for a change. And they discussed the various programs that I could be a part of, counseling, drug dependency programs, and I said, yes, yes, whatever you think is best for me. And then they asked for my address and I gave them the number of the hotel in Uptown I had just moved to a few days before. And they came back and they said "We're sorry, you live outside our jurisdiction so you are not eligible for any sort of discount which means you have to pay the full price and it is obvious with your employment history that you cannot." And I said, "But I lived within your jurisdiction just a few days ago, and I may very well live there again next week." And they said, "We're sorry, but you'll have to go somewhere else, perhaps to Illinois Masonic." And I asked "But I'll have to go through all these questions again?" And they said "Yes." And so I picked up my coat and said "Thank you anyway." And I left and I can't bring myself to go anywhere else...

...pangs and pangs, wherever there is a hollow are silly receptacles for nostalgia. Old people who eat alone make me cry, it's this curse of mine, to cry in public like that, i can't help myself sometimes. i love old radio shows. i love places i've never been. maybe i radiate outward. sometimes i am sure my face is glowing with a curious fever, but people won't take two looks at me and think "She's ill." They'll murmur instead "She looks like she's on fire" and then i'll explode...


PROPYLACTIC RAG


so i was at the hiv clinic for a second test, a six month follow up, and i got the same counselor as from before, this nice guy named guy. this time there was a young black woman too, a trainee, and guy said She'll Be Sitting With Us. so for our session, he made it a point of making it a good one, and once again he stressed the importance of using rubbers and bleaching your needles and once again he asked me Do You Know How To Put On A Rubber and i said Of Course I Do, and he asked Have You Ever Done It Before. and i said Of Course I Have. but this time he wanted to know more and he said How. Show Us. and i had to describe it with my hands not knowing the correct vocabulary for this situation. and of course i forgot about the part about pinching the nipple of the rubber to make sure no air gets in there otherwise the rubber could very well break. and guy said Well Why Don't You Demonstrate So That We Know You Know How To Do It and he turns to the trainee and says Go Get The Dildo and i'm thinking O Brother. and she brings back this huge black rubber latex heavy duty cock and balls ensemble and i'm thinking Goodness. and for god's sake in my demonstration i don't even open the package right and i rip the first rubber. and then they must have given me an extra large dildo or else an extra small rubber cuz i had troubles getting the silly thing on. in fact i could barely get my fist around that thing thank you.


IF THE BODY IS A TEMPLE THEN WE ARE IN RUINS

Blow out after blow out – I try to explain. About how people only want you when you're good, and we all know how I got a fifty fifty chance on that lottery ticket. It's not like I set out to do it all on purpose. It just has to do with Expectations, you know, and how hard it is to live up to them. It has nothing to do with light or love or loyalty. It's more like: when I fall off a horse I don't get back on it I send it to the glue factory. Am I good for nothing save a hell summer pallor, yellow of ashes. A figure cuts across the boulevards with a sudden hunger food sex or drugs can't reach. And not even nights full of dreams of nothing can satisfy or recall.

DREAM In some part of time north of here, distorted by existence: She was there too, the other my lover say fit to conquer because he was feeling so insecure. In this dream I am on a journey. Now I am confused.; yellow churning water and metal in my ears? I am accompanied at all times with a desire for a gun and a heavy presence in my right breast. As night falls, green goes first, and I am stranded in a black part of town, in an empty place. The buildings are all large empty warehouses and many of them are scarred by boards and the scorch of arson. Black men come at me all night long with razors they carry like silver in their hands. A station wagon full of young blonde students drives through but they are too weak to do anything. World travelers since they were young, they're too scared to even get out of their car. And so I am on my own. But she was there, though she may have been too busy saving her own life to think about me. But I think of her all the time. Finally, I am saved by morning. Not the zombie dawn of an all night fall; when the sun rises solid all the blackmen immediately raced into the brickwork. I am thrown into the air as though I were flying, the air which is now green and gold. I m flying over lush green countryside. I was so high the earth was a vast thing beneath me.

POST NO BILLS

blow, no pills, glow, no frills, slow, for thrills: aahh, you guys slay me. lissen to us all... it's a sunday in chicago and i'm living at the ymca and somebody, Some Body, has the sense to play the blues on an old radio where it belongs. get it? BBKing says, "Remember, everybody's got the blues."

but it's not that either. since last weekend... iggy pop played at the metro tuesday night but of course i can't afford 20 a pop just for a ticket in – so then hanging around out front who do i run into but a major blast from the past – the one man my X would kill me if he found out crossed my path, but like the black cat that i am or like to be, i let him. yes, yes. so he used to be a cowboy to me in my wild eyed youth – having first learned the Art of Scam or Be Scammed from this man having been taken for quite the emotional ride – not counting the 90 m.p.h. alley rides in any borrowed car – Acid nights aside he was/still is/fearless. fearless, but a little... ah, dumb. there he is and his name is joe.

a real bad cup of coffee. i was right and I was wrong. in this state called 1 AM it doesn't matter much now, how crazy I had been for him – so there he is no longer the cowboy in my poems but sporting jesus hair and beard, irish choir boy gone wrong – he's still got his big black boots, and now he's leading around a dog, a deaf white pitbull named stinky who i guess because she can't hear never figured it out that pitbulls are supposed to be fierce and fearsome. she obviously loves joe a lot. most dogs do. so he makes a pass – i've changed so much from the girl who didn't know much but expected a lot – even the bones in my face have shifted into something more defined. he's not at all sure it's me – but when he figures it out he's glad enough. anything is better than being alone...

of course there's no accounting for this grudge i can't get rid of. so we're talking about the fire escape and maybe later when this latino looking dude walks up, real chollo like in chino and T and sweat bandana – joe knows him and i've seen him around comparing tattoos – he has 'dreamer' in cursive on his neck, prison peacock on bicep, various vargas replicas on forearms. he wants to know from joe where he can get some (whisper) BOMB. joe knows and a short time and trickster basehead black as a spade through and through later, mission accomplished – and i find out i got the hots for chollo bandito from LA but irish from mt. prospect – hey we all gotta tell a story somehow. who cares if it's not always true...

later at the lake i'm turning circles, happy circles. wayne's gone and the deaf pitbull keeps running off. there's no point in calling after her she can't hear. joe and i meet some nu waves blowing frosted one hitters in their honda – i'm about to go out as it goes, like complete in sleep, deliciously, like i like it. the nu waves make some crack about the ring in my nose and so i flash the extra large one in my nipple as they're driving away. suddenly hoe's interested in me again: Damn, how cum ya didn't show me that before. i was saving it baby, and he's grabbing my ass now like he useta never – like all illusions and allusions, i think i'm in such control cuz HE CAN'T TOUCH ME, no matter how much my flesh is kneaded, poked, prodded. no matter how dark i got under.

back at his squatter's apartment we do one last baby speedball at which point i take off all my clothes and pretend i am all of five years old jumping up and down on the naked mattress. really, he was game for that all right...

but now the sun is coming up and he still ain't cum yet. he won't give it up. for four hours now he's been saying: I'm almost there. I'm almost there. lissen: you ain't nowhere. in and out of my sweaty dream, sun comes up. and i like that i can think about anything and anybody i want, thinking of wayne, thinking of the rush. finally to joe though i got to say – enough already i'm raw meat, huh, and surely he knows that he is not with who he thinks he is, cuz he knew me way back when, when i only was, and now I AM. i like it this way, but i really wish he'd get off me.

and now i get this infection. typical. stuffing yogurt up my wangthang to get some relief. lissening to blues on a Sunday in my room at the y...

## SEX AND DEATH AND FEAR (THE RAW DEAL)

Beyond distance I imagine talking fast and furious to swallow all this space between us, young and risking: about those blue pills and the monday night blow out with those fetid artjunkies, the couple from the Club. I did confess, didn't I? I reacted like a trained rat to the sight of those two little perfect blue ovals not realizing how dangerous they were. Thorazine.

Psychoactive. The woman who gave them to me said they were given to her so she could sleep. That was the magic word. The directions called for a dose of two. I took ten. I couldn't move, so to speak, for about 3 days. Nerves buzzed, I twitched a lot. Constant metal squirming. Wanting to concentrate. Wanting to move from under the weight of No Response. In a chair of elocution, it was fucken torture. And then to further damage my self, I let that Boy touch me, the one who was always hanging around. If only he had just gotten it over with, but no, he tries to take me into consideration which was the last thing I wanted or needed...

DREAM JakeLabotts and I were riding around nighttime in some small town, the black as black countryside somewhere east of here unknown. We were looking to score. With us in the van were 3 others, a couple with a child, old friends of mine, and a black girl I had never seen before. Back at the ranch we fixed and fixed for that is the nature of the drug we are doing. The whole process was one of extreme frustration because the needle i was using kept breaking off or bending in my arm causing me to miss my shot sometimes. Or else the needle would grow larger or smaller. Like in some kinda weird alice in LaLaLand feeling so inept I kept at it, gritting my teeth, swearing and ready to kill. That too is the nature of the drug. Finally it comes down to the last blast and I'm jonesin to make it a good one, a good one that would smoke my toes and put bells to ringing in my ears. One that would lead me to hear the second hand on the universal clock. But what do I do but blow out my shot by adding too much water, so much so that the plunger is drawn almost all the way back not leaving much room to go in for the kill. But I tie off anyway, Jake's sitting beside me, and I fix that needle pointing in the right direction, but the needle keeps bending. One breaks off in my arm, wiggling there like a little maggot. So I'm forced to run around the ranch trying to find another one and start the whole process over again. Finally I find a vein and I hit and I'm pushing the plunger in for what seems like an awfully long time and by then I'm so pissed off by this whole scene I rip the damned thing out of my arm catching the needle on something vital, I guess, cuz when I pull out a long string like red spaghetti vein follows. Suddenly, in a dream that previously had been strictly black and white, everything is red, like technicolor, and there's blood gushing out of my arm like a geyser. The baby is lying on the floor and when I stand up and extra strong pulse comes up and the baby is covered with blood. Standing up, I'm feeling a little faint, swaying, I say to Jake "Jake I think I fucked up big time this time." Real calm like, I'm not trying to panic, it's just a dream after all. And the black girl is screaming at the top of some stairs and I say to Jake "Jake, I think I better go to the hospital and quick" but even as I say I remember that darkness out there and how we're in the middle of the absolute Nowheresville, like, way the fuck out in the boonies. And I think, well, if I don't stop this flow of blood I'm gonna die, and I think, yeah, this is it.

## Mythmaking: I Am All
## (for Lydia Lunch)

and none
of these things: a woman
a stone, a low keen moan
roaming the mother load, diva
on the receiving edge, a privilege
privy to piles of pathetic pilgrims
praying for the sigh that will lay them
down dead. alabaster babble with a luster
of luscious lust. the rust of a million
useless mouths; I am the prelude
to smooth rudeness, a new spoor
clinging to the door of whoredom
where you jerk to the sameness
of the fixed pout
I sing glass
missing throat, flight of cairo
o ye bride of the dead forgotten
saved in tombs
dancing tattooed thighs
in a rotting world
I am the fetid word, here and herbaceous
fertile as the fall from your flailing feet
polyethylene has nothing on me
the grand harpooness, a spark waiting
to mouth off in tongues the hurry up come
I am not a missive of submissiveness
but a weapon of torrential possibilities
So when you kiss my darkening face
o you lover of leavened needs
you with your warped visions of sameness
your fists of material drivel
don't say my name for fear
don't say you know it
for behind the navel is a veil
and once danced with
will leave your vain clutchings with nothing

Photo of Lorri Jackson by Fred Burkhart
Property of Larry Oberc, used with permission

NAME (Print) Lorri Jackson

Social Security #

Fall ◯ Spring ◯
Summer ☐
1984-1985

**Columbia College**
600 S. Michigan Ave., Chica
(312) 663-160

*An Acknowledgement*

*Projects like this are never solitary endeavors. It would be too much for two hands and one pair of eyes. So, first, thanks to Joani Reese for her last-minute, inspired, buzzer-beating assistance with the finished product.*

*Then there's Larry Oberc, who was my "art guy" at the Fiction Review. Larry has championed Lorri's work for over two decades and produced biographical work on her life in several magazines over the years. He never failed to pitch in whenever I needed him.*

*And, most of all, Leann Jackson Bigos. Because without her persistence, patience, and loyalty to her sister, the book in your hands – sanctioned by the Jackson family – simply does not exist.*

*RW*

Made in the USA
San Bernardino, CA
13 May 2017